# Contents

iv   Contents

**Access to History**

General Editor: Keith Randell

# The Unification of Italy, 1815-1870

## Andrina Stiles

Hodder & Stoughton

A MEMBER OF THE HODDER HEADLINE GROUP

The cover illustration shows a portrait of Garibaldi by Filippo Palizzi (Courtesy Scala)

Some other titles in the series:

**France: Monarchy, Republic and Empire 1814–70**
Keith Randell                                                    ISBN 0 340 51805 7
**France: The Third Republic**
Keith Randell                                                    ISBN 0 340 55569 6
**The Unification of Germany**
Andrina Stiles                                                   ISBN 0 340 51810 3
**The Concert of Europe: International Relations 1815–70**
John Lowe                                                        ISBN 0 340 53496 6
**Rivalry and Accord: International Relations 1870–1914**
John Lowe                                                        ISBN 0 340 51806 5
**Russia 1815–51**
Russell Sherman                                                  ISBN 0 340 54789 8
**Reaction and Revolutions: Russia 1881–1924**
Michael Lynch                                                    ISBN 0 340 53336 6
**Italy: Liberalism and Fascism 1870–1945**
Mark Robson                                                      ISBN 0 340 54548 8

*British Library Cataloguing in Publication Data*
Stiles, Andrina
    The unification of Italy 1815–1870.
    (Access to history)
    1. Italy–Politics and government
    I. Title    II. Series
    945'.08    DG551
ISBN 0 340 51809 X

First published in Access to A-Level History series 1986 four impressions.
This edition published 1989
Impression number 10   9   8   7   6   5
Year                   1999   1998   1997   1996   1995   1994

Printed in Great Britain for Hodder & Stoughton Educational, a division of Hodder Headline Plc, 338 Euston Road, London NW1 3BH by Page Bros, Norwich

# Preface

## To the general reader

Although the *Access to History* series has been designed with the needs of students studying the subject at higher examination levels very much in mind, it also has a great deal to offer the general reader. The main body of the text (i.e. ignoring the Study Guides at the ends of chapters) forms a readable and yet stimulating survey of a coherent topic as studied by historians. However, each author's aim has not merely been to provide a clear explanation of what happened in the past (to interest and inform): it has also been assumed that most readers wish to be stimulated into thinking further about the topic and to form opinions of their own about the significance of the events that are described and discussed (to be challenged). Thus, although no prior knowledge of the topic is expected on the reader's part, she or he is treated as an intelligent and thinking person throughout. The author tends to share ideas and possibilities with the reader, rather than passing on numbers of so-called 'historical truths'.

## To the student reader

There are many ways in which the series can be used by students studying History at a higher level. It will, therefore, be worthwhile thinking about your own study strategy before you start your work on this book. Obviously, your strategy will vary depending on the aim you have in mind, and the time for study that is available to you.

If, for example, you want to acquire a general overview of the topic in the shortest possible time, the following approach will probably be the most effective:

1. Read Chapter 1 and think about its contents.
2. Read the 'Making notes' section at the end of Chapter 2 and decide whether it is necessary for you to read this chapter.
3. If it is, read the chapter, stopping at each heading or * to note down the main points that have been made.
4. Repeat stage 2 (and stage 3 where appropriate) for all the other chapters.

If, however, your aim is to gain a thorough grasp of the topic, taking however much time is necessary to do so, you may benefit from carrying out the same procedure with each chapter, as follows:

1. Read the chapter as fast as you can, and preferably at one sitting.
2. Study the flow diagram at the end of the chapter, ensuring that you understand the general 'shape' of what you have just read.
3. Read the 'Making notes' section (and the 'Answering essay

questions' section, if there is one) and decide what further work you need to do on the chapter. In particularly important sections of the book, this will involve reading the chapter a second time and stopping at each heading and * to think about (and to write a summary of) what you have just read.

4. Attempt the 'Source-based questions' section. It will sometimes be sufficient to think through your answers, but additional understanding will often be gained by forcing yourself to write them down.

When you have finished the main chapters of the book, study the 'Further Reading' section and decide what additional reading (if any) you will do on the topic.

This book has been designed to help make your studies both enjoyable and successful. If you can think of ways in which this could have been done more effectively, please write to tell me. In the meantime, I hope that you will gain greatly from your study of History.

Keith Randell

# Introduction

In parts of Western Europe nation states had developed in the centuries before 1815. France, Britain and Spain, in particular, had developed as unified kingdoms with a single government controlling territory populated by peoples who shared strong cultural and linguistic traditions. Similar, although not identical, bases for nationhood existed in Italy and Germany. Yet in 1815 these areas remained politically divided.

In the following chapters, the sequence of events which resulted in Italy becoming a unified nation state is described and discussed. As the book is read thought should be given to a number of questions. First and foremost, clear answers to the question, 'What was the general pattern of events in Italy between 1815 and 1871?', must be established. Look at the chart on page 5. Three stages in the story of Italian unification should be apparent. The first stage is largely concerned with the failure of attempts to alter the political structure of Italy. You need to understand what was attempted and the reasons for failure. Chapter 1 deals with these issues. Chapters 2, 3, 4 and 5 consider the personalities and events of the stages of initial unification and consolidation. As you read these chapters you should identify facts and arguments that will help you to reach conclusions about the reasons why initial failure was followed by success. How much was this because of the actions of named individuals? How much was it the result of general changes in the political, economic and social situation? The section which follows should help to establish in your mind the major issues you will be expected to be able to discuss once you have completed your study of the unification of Italy.

---

*Introducing essay questions on 'The Unification of Italy 1815–71'*

Essay questions on 'The Unification of Italy' tend to fall into two main categories: those demanding a knowledge of the whole period 1815–1871, or a very substantial part of it, and those concentrating on particular individuals or specific topics. You need to be prepared to answer both types of question.

In this section you will find examples of the wider and more general questions. It will be helpful to keep in mind the main issues raised by these questions as you read through the book. Further discussion of these general questions will be found on pages 92–3, to which you should turn after working through all five chapters. Typical questions on particular topics will be found at the end of Chapters 1, 2, 3 and 4.

Each general question can be placed under one of three main headings:

1  What were the obstacles to unification? How were they overcome?
2  Why did nationalism at first fail? and later succeed?

3  Did Italy unite herself? or did she need outside help?

Notice that each 'issue' is made up of two closely related questions. Typical 'what obstacles' questions are:

> 'What were the main obstacles in the way of Italian unification?' (Scottish, 1982)
> 'What were the chief obstacles to Italian unification and how far had they been removed by 1861?' (AEB, 1982)
> 'What were the main obstacles to Italian liberation and unification? Analyse the stages by which these obstacles were surmounted in the years 1850–70' (SUJB, 1985)

Questions of this kind invite you to make a list of difficulties in the way of Italian unification and then to show how/whether they were overcome. As you read through the book look out for these difficulties and for their solutions. It would be worthwhile making a list of them on a separate sheet of paper as you come across them.

This also applies to questions about the reasons for the initial failure and the final success of Italian nationalism.

Typical questions on this issure are:

> 'Explain why Italian nationalism failed in 1848–9, but succeeded by 1871' (Scottish, 1981)
> 'What were the lessons of 1848–9 for those interested in Italian liberation and unification? How well were the lessons learned?' (Cambridge, 1982)

The third group of general questions asks you about the relative importance of Italian efforts and other factors in the achievement of unification.

A typical question is:

> 'How much did outside influence affect the unification of Italy?' (Oxford and Cambridge, 1979)

Questions on this issue often embody a quotation and may be presented as 'challenging statements'. You will find a discussion on how to answer questions of this kind on pages 92–3.

# CHAPTER 1
# Italy 1815–1852

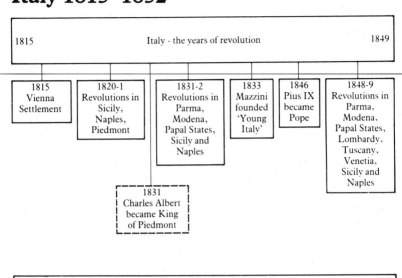

| 1815 | Italy - the years of revolution | 1849 |
|---|---|---|

| 1815 Vienna Settlement | 1820-1 Revolutions in Sicily, Naples, Piedmont | 1831-2 Revolutions in Parma, Modena, Papal States, Sicily and Naples | 1833 Mazzini founded 'Young Italy' | 1846 Pius IX became Pope | 1848-9 Revolutions in Parma, Modena, Papal States, Lombardy, Tuscany, Venetia, Sicily and Naples |

1831
Charles Albert became King of Piedmont

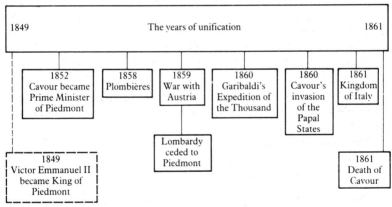

| 1849 | The years of unification | 1861 |
|---|---|---|

| 1852 Cavour became Prime Minister of Piedmont | 1858 Plombières | 1859 War with Austria | 1860 Garibaldi's Expedition of the Thousand | 1860 Cavour's invasion of the Papal States | 1861 Kingdom of Italy |

1849
Victor Emmanuel II became King of Piedmont

Lombardy ceded to Piedmont

1861
Death of Cavour

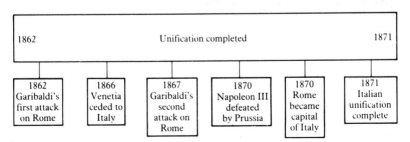

| 1862 | Unification completed | 1871 |
|---|---|---|

| 1862 Garibaldi's first attack on Rome | 1866 Venetia ceded to Italy | 1867 Garibaldi's second attack on Rome | 1870 Napoleon III defeated by Prussia | 1870 Rome became capital of Italy | 1871 Italian unification complete |

*Summary – The unification of Italy, 1815–70*

## 1 The Italian States

In April 1796 the French armies of Napoleon I invaded northern Italy and by 1799 had conquered the whole mainland. Apart from a few months, they remained in control until 1814 of the whole peninsula except Venetia, the area round Venice, which had been given to Austria. The French occupation had far reaching effects on Italy. The power of the Church and of the Pope was reduced, changes were made in landownership and land was redistributed. A new middle class began to appear. Agriculture was improved and the peasants were freed from their old feudal ties and obligations. But the French did not want competition from Italian manufactured goods. They just wanted Italian raw materials, such as silk, for their own home industries, so Italian industry remained undeveloped. A start was made on improving communications within the peninsula with new roads being built across the Alps and the Appenines. Italian laws were standardised and French civil and commercial legal codes were introduced. Equally important, the French introduced representative government in to Italy. Elected assemblies were provided on the French model. These constitutional developments gave the new Italian middle class a chance for political discussion and action.

State boundaries were rearranged a number of times during the Napoleonic era, ending up with a division of the peninsula into only three parts. One third, including Piedmont, was annexed to France, one third became the Kingdom of Italy, and the remainder was ruled by Napoleon's brother, Joseph, as the Kingdom of Naples.

All these changes gave some encouragement to Italian nationalism. The French gave Italy a modicum of unity, at first by force of conquest, and later through legal reforms and the introduction of political changes on a national basis. This national unity might have been artificial and imposed from outside but at least it existed, so much so that in the chaos of 1815 the King of Naples could call on the people of the whole peninsula to support him and to make Italy a united and independent state. He got little help, but the fact that he felt able to make such an appeal showed that the idea of Italy as a nation state was considered to be a realistic possibility.

* Napoleon I himself had said, 'Italy is one nation. Unity of customs, language and literature must at a period more or less distant unite her inhabitants under one government, and Rome without doubt will be chosen by the Italians as their capital.' But in 1815 it was a long time ahead, for the Vienna Settlement of that year, drawn up by the Great Powers of Russia, Austria, Prussia and Britain, redrew the map of Italy so it resembled the Italy of pre-Napoleonic times (see map, page 7). It also restored the eighteenth-century political situation by reinstating most of the ruling families which had been dispossessed during the

See Preface for explanation of * symbol.

*Italy in 1815*

French occupation. These 'restored monarchs' quickly re-established themselves as absolute rulers in their respective states. The Great Powers had two aims in Italy in 1815. One was to prevent any possible attempt by France to gain control of the country at a future date. The other was to suppress revolutionary or nationalist movements which might be a danger to established governments. Both these aims were achieved by making sure that Austria could control the Italian peninsula effectively. This was done by putting Lombardy and Venetia, the rich and strategically important parts of northern Italy, under the direct rule of the Austrian Emperor in Vienna. Austrian predominance in Italy was reinforced by installing members of the Austrian Imperial family, the Habsburgs, as the ruling sovereigns of most other Italian states. The King of Piedmont was a cousin of the Emperor, as were the Dukes of Modena and the Duke of Tuscany; an aunt was Queen of Naples, while another aunt was Duchess of Parma.

* Liberal ideas had been gaining ground in Europe since the end of the eighteenth century. Metternich, the Austrian Chancellor (Chief Minister) was totally opposed to them. Liberals believed that the people had a right to some say in government and that this was best achieved by a representative assembly or parliament, elected by property owners. They were concerned with establishing a rule of law which guaranteed certain rights, such as a fair trial, and certain freedoms, such as freedom of speech, to all citizens. They favoured constitutional monarchy as the best form of government for they feared equally the two political extremes of absolute monarchy and republican democracy. Both of these they believed were a threat to their political, economic and social position, for most liberals were middle class.

* Their moderate, non-violent policy was in contrast with that of the radicals, the extremists, who wanted social reforms and a redistribution of wealth and were prepared to use revolutionary means to obtain them. The radicals believed that political power should lie with the people not with parliament (the 'sovereignty of the people' not the 'sovereignty of parliament'). Any representative assembly would have to be elected by a universal franchise giving the vote to all men over 25 not just the property owners as the liberals wished. However, liberals and radicals were united in their opposition to the 'restored monarchies' reintroduced in 1815.

* Metternich was opposed to nationalism as well as liberalism. Nationalists believed that people of the same race, language, culture and tradition should be united in an independent nation of their own. It should have clear geographical boundaries and not be under the control of any other people. Metternich had no intention of allowing such dangerous ideas to develop in Italy, where they would be a threat to Austrian control. He believed that Austrian safety depended on the maintenance of the eighteenth-century status quo in Italy, with separate states ruled by absolute monarchs.

There was no suggestion at the Congress of Vienna of establishing an

Italian Confederation under the control of Austria, as had been done in Germany. Although he did not make it until 30 years later, Metternich's famous remark that 'Italy is only a geographical expression' accurately described the Italy of 1815. 'Italian affairs do not exist', Metternich did say in 1815. 'Italy' as a nation did not exist, only the jigsaw of Naples, Piedmont, Tuscany and the other Italian states. There were no 'Italians' but only Neapolitans, Piedmontese, Tuscans and the rest, and that, as far as Metternich was concerned, was how it should, and would, stay.

He was not the only one to think this, for even the intelligent and well educated saw nothing but difficulties in the way of unity between the states. The Piedmontese ambassador to Russia wrote about the annexation of Genoa by Piedmont:

1   . . . The acquisition of Genoa will have danger for us. The union of nations encounters no difficulties on the map, but in reality it is a different matter; there are peoples who cannot be mixed; perhaps the Piedmontese and Genoans fall into this class, separated as they
5  are by an ancient and ingrained hatred. Where will the capital be? and where unity?

In 1815 local loyalties were more important than dreams of national unity.

  * At the restoration of the old regime in Italy, the Pope was among those who regained their positions. During the Napoleonic occupation successive Popes had been taken into exile in France, and the temporal power of the Pope as ruler of an Italian state had been declared at an end. But when the Pope returned he was intent on restoring temporal, as well as spiritual control. The Papal States were divided into seventeen provinces, five of which were under the authority of Papal Legates, or Cardinals, who acted as provincial governors. The remainder, which were nearer Rome, were controlled by priests known as Delegates. The whole administration of the Papal States was in the hands of the clergy. The lay people had no part in government, apart from a few lay members of advisory bodies called 'congregations'.

One of the most reactionary of the restored monarchies was that of Piedmont in north-west Italy. There the French legal systems were abolished, nobles were given back their lands and former positions, and even the use of the roads built by the French was actively discouraged. In Sicily, in the south of Italy, the King of Naples cancelled the constitution which had been granted in 1812, and declared that the two parts of his kingdom would henceforth be governed as one. There was opposition from small groups of liberals and radicals on the island, both demanding constitutions of a very moderate kind. The liberals wanted a two-chamber parliament, one chamber to be hereditary and the other to be elected on a very restricted franchise. Even the radicals only wanted a single indirectly elected chamber, through which the King would rule. These demands were turned down, but similar efforts to obtain constitutions led to the outbreak of revolutions in several states in 1820–1 and 1831–2.

* In 1820 revolutions broke out in Naples, Sicily and Piedmont and in all of them secret societies played an important part. These societies probably had their origins in eighteenth-century Freemasonary, where men formed themselves into groups pledged to mutual protection with secret passwords and semi-religious rituals. The Catholic Church viewed these associations with extreme suspicion and denounced them as heretical as well as a danger to the established social order. By the late 1790s other similar groups had arisen throughout Italy which were dedicated to driving out the French invader. After 1815 their aim was to overthrow the restored monarchs and to drive out the Austrians.

The societies attracted a wide variety of members, mostly army officers, students, lawyers, teachers and doctors, all well educated and nearly all middle class. A few enlightened noblemen were to be found in the societies, but peasants or workers were almost unknown. The majority of members were patriotic, enthusiastic and daring; many were idealists, some were dreamers, a few were rogues and criminals. Their strength lay in their heroism, their willingness to risk their lives in wild ventures and impossible tasks. Their weakness lay in their lack of co-ordinated action and their equal lack of practical organisation. There were a number of different secret societies, sometimes working together and sometimes on their own. The members were in small groups scattered throughout Italy. Because of the great secrecy in which they operated historians are not sure in most cases what their aims were, nor how effective their work really was.

Far and away the best known and most important of the societies were the *Carbonari*. They were in existence in 1807 but their origin is uncertain. The name means 'charcoal burners' and it has been suggested that the earliest members were men who sold charcoal for domestic fuel. They were particularly active in Southern Italy, especially in Naples, where they are thought to have numbered about 60 000. This probably represents around 5 per cent of the adult male population and by 1816 the government of Naples was sufficiently worried to order the suppression of the society. Their efforts failed and the *Carbonari* rapidly increased in strength. The members practised elaborate rituals and had to swear unquestioning obedience to their leaders. In theory they were an international society with headquarters in Paris, but they were most active in Italy. Unlike many of the other societies they were not particularly anti-Catholic, and while planning armed revolution and the overthrow of the existing social order, were not committed to republicanism. The *Carbonari* as a whole do not in fact seem to have had very clearly defined aims. It was left to individual groups to decide their own particular policies and methods. In Piedmont, for example, they hoped to establish a constitutional monarchy, and even in Naples they did not want to replace the King with a republic but simply to obtain a constitution from him.

## 2 The Revolutions of 1820

The 1820 revolutions began in Naples. By 1818 the restored King Ferdinand had greatly increased the power of the Church. It was given authority to censor any publications with which it disagreed. This angered the professional middle classes, the lawyers and teachers, because it made freedom of expression impossible. Ferdinand was also in great financial difficulties, and the government cut back on public expenditure, halted work on roads and harbours, and reduced still further what little educational provision there was. Everywhere there was poverty, corrupt government and restriction on personal freedom.

In Sicily the forced union with Naples had not been a happy one. The government in Naples had taken little notice of local Sicilian feelings and paid little attention to Sicilian needs. Agricultural prices had fallen sharply, and the effect on the Sicilian economy had been disastrous. All social classes were affected, but particularly the peasants, who became more impoverished and ever deeper in debt.

News of a revolution in Spain in January 1820 stirred the liberals of Naples into action. Led by a priest and supported by 100 non-commissioned officers and soldiers from the cavalry, 30 *Carbonari* advanced on the town of Avellino. They quickly gained popular support, and a widespread uprising developed. The attempt by the government troops to round up the rebels was very halfhearted, and the actions of one of the divisional commanders actually ensured the success of the rising. The commander, General Pepe, led one infantry and two cavalry regiments to join the rebels, and put himself at the head of what was now a revolution.

The following day, 6 July, King Ferdinand promised to issue a constitution within a week. But the revolutionaries did not trust him and they began to demand that the constitution should be the same as the one granted to Spain in 1812. This Spanish constitution had given the vote to all adult males to elect a single-chamber parliament. The King agreed, subject to certain possible changes to be decided later by an elected assembly. The revolutionaries marched into the city of Naples without opposition, Pepe was received by the King and the revolution appeared to have succeeded without a single death or injury.

A new government was appointed, Pepe was put in charge of the army and the King swore to defend the constitution. The *Carbonari* gained large numbers of recruits when rumours circulated that they were going to redistribute all land to the peasants and reform the Church.

* Meanwhile in Sicily a separate revolutionary movement had started. It was less concerned with ideas of national unity, than with separation from Naples. Led by the *maestranze*, the trade guilds and fuelled by news of the revolution in Naples, there were riots in Palermo, Sicily's capital. Demands were made for a constitution, government offices were burned down and prisoners released. The revolutionaries, headed by the guild representatives, took over in Palermo, and the Neapolitan governor left

for home by boat.

When the newly elected Parliament met for the first time in Naples in October 1820 it consisted of middle-class professional men, together with a few priests and noblemen. They discussed events in Sicily and decided to reinforce the government troops on the island to restore Neapolitan authority and to suppress the revolutionaries, whose radical excesses they viewed with horror and suspicion. They had no intention of allowing Sicily to declare independence. The Two Sicilies must remain united and Neapolitan control must be maintained by force.

* Metternich was concerned by the success of the revolution in Naples, for he believed peace could best be preserved by maintaining the status quo and by suppressing revolution wherever it occurred. He argued that what happened inside one state may have an unsettling effect on other states. This entitled them to take notice of and, if necessary take action against unwelcome events in the neighbouring state. So he developed the system of holding international congresses, meetings of the Great Powers, to discuss problems, consider action and maintain peace. In 1820 such a congress was held at Troppau. As a result of this, Austria, Prussia and Russia agreed that the Great Powers should interfere, by force if necessary, to restore any government which had been overthrown by revolution.

Naples was not specifically mentioned, but was clearly in Metternich's mind. In 1821 the King of Naples was invited to attend a Congress at Laibach to discuss affairs in his kingdom. Safely away from Naples, he declared that he had been forced to grant the constitution out of fear, and asked for Austrian intervention. The request delighted Metternich, and despite a brave resistance by the Neapolitan army under General Pepe, the Austrian's entered the city of Naples in March 1821. Severe repression followed. Arrests, imprisonment and executions were meted out equally to liberals loyal to the monarchy who had simply wanted a constitution, and to republican extremists who had wanted to alter the whole structure of society. Even Metternich was shocked by the savagery, and intervened to secure the dismissal of the reactionary police chief.

* The other area of revolution in 1820 was Piedmont. The restored monarchy of Victor Emmanuel I had destroyed nearly all evidence of the years of French occupation including the French legal system. Equality before the law was abandoned and the right to a free and open trial abolished. A royal edict declared that the constitution of Piedmont was that laid down in 1770, and that it could not be changed. Piedmont was an absolute monarchy, and remained so, despite pressure from a small group of middle-class liberals in the years between 1815 and 1820.

When news of the revolution in Naples in July 1820 reached Piedmont, membership of the *Carbonari* increased rapidly. There was discontent in the University of Turin, where in January 1821 a group of revolutionary students staged a sit-in and were violently removed by the police. There was discontent too in the army, and at Alessandria in March a group of revolutionary officers were joined by middle-class liberals in a take-over of the fortress. They established a revolutionary government in the town and proclaimed their independence as the 'Kingdom of Italy'. They then declared war on Austria. Another army mutiny, this time in Turin, encouraged Victor Emmanuel to abdicate a few days later. Liberal hopes that he might be persuaded to grant a constitution and lead a war against Austria to free Lombardy had never been very realistic. They now had to be abandoned.

The liberals turned, therefore, to the young Charles Albert, second in line to the throne, for leadership. He issued a vague proclamation referring to the Spanish Constitution of 1812 as a 'law of state', except for any modifications which might be made later. Victor Emmanuel's brother and heir, Charles Felix, was absent from Piedmont on a visit to Modena. Charles Albert therefore took control and appointed a new government. But a message speedily arrived from Charles Felix denouncing Charles Albert as a rebel and refusing to accept any change 'in the form of government'. Charles Albert took fright and fled from Turin, which was left in the hands of the liberals. They prepared to fight to defend the constitution which Charles Albert had granted, while Charles Felix appealed to Metternich for Austrian intervention. Austrian troops were sent into Piedmont and, together with troops loyal to Charles Felix, they defeated the revolutionary forces from Turin. Hundreds of revolutionaries went into exile. The revolution was over. Absolutism was again supreme in Piedmont, backed up until 1823 by an Austrian occupying army.

## 3 The Revolutions of 1831

In 1831 revolution again broke out in Italy and again the impetus was a foreign revolution, not in Spain this time, but in France, where the July Revolution had taken place the previous year. Italian liberals now cherished the idea that France would support Italian revolutions, and risings with largely constitutional aims took place in Modena, Parma and the Papal States.

* In Modena the conspiracy was masterminded by Enrico Misley, the son of a university professor. Since his student days in the early 1820s Misley had been intriguing to bring about a more united Italy with constitutional forms of government. He pinned his hopes on his local ruler, Duke Francesco IV of Modena, but his trust was betrayed. Francesco went along with Misley in order to find out what the plotters intended, but revealed his hand at the last moment and arrested the conspirators two days before their uprising was due to break out in February 1831.

Thinking that the danger was passed, Francesco went to Vienna to negotiate help should he be troubled by revolutionaries from beyond his frontiers. While he was away, revolutionaries from the districts around Modena banded together, took over the city, and formed a provisional government. In neighbouring Parma students, encouraged by events in Modena, organized a series of riots and demanded a constitution. The ruler of Parma, the Duchess Marie-Louise, fled in terror and a provisional government was established. Contacts with Modena were immediately forged and a joint army commander was appointed. But the revolutionaries were given little time to organize themselves. Within a month Duke Francesco had returned at the head of loyal troops, and had defeated his opponents. Savage reprisals were taken, and everyone suspected of supporting the rebels was imprisoned, exiled or executed. Even a moustache or beard could lead to a man's arrest on suspicion of being a revolutionary.

Similar uprisings took place in the Papal States, largely organized by members of the professional classes who resented the oppressive rule of the Church authorities. The government provided little resistance and a provisional government, giving itself the title of 'The Government of the Italian Provinces' was formed in Bologna in February 1831. But it also had a very brief existence. Austrian troops moved in and rapidly defeated the rebels. During the remainder of 1831 and the early months of 1832 further uprisings took place throughout the Papal States but they were savagely suppressed by the largely violent and indisciplined Papal troops.

* The revolutions of 1820 and 1831 had achieved very little. In Piedmont, Naples and the Papal States reactionary government strengthened its hold. Austria still provided help and support for absolute governments in difficulty and seemed likely to continue to do so, by military intervention where necessary. Naples had successfully reimposed control over Sicily, and made a future break-away less likely by abolishing the trade guilds which had been the basis of the revolution there. Where revolutions were successful in ousting their rulers, the success was only temporary, and was due less to the strength of the revolutionaries than to the failure of the governments, and to their inadequate resources. With the French Revolution still fresh in their minds, the rulers expected to be defeated.

The revolutions had been weakened by being parochial, concerned only with separate and limited areas. There was little communication between the revolutionaries in the different states and even less co-operation. The revolutionary government in Bologna refused to send help to Modena. They took the statement of non-intervention issued by the French government of Louis-Philippe, 'We do not recognize the right of any people to force us to fight in its cause; the blood of Frenchmen belongs to France alone', to mean that it would be equally wrong for one group of Italian revolutionaries to send help to another group in a different Italian state.

The revolutionary movements were ill co-ordinated. They relied very much on the network of small groups of revolutionaries set up by the *Carbonari* and the other secret societies, but these were isolated units and their aims differed from place to place. Most revolutionaries were very moderate and not given to violence; usually all that they were trying to achieve was the introduction of a constitution to allow some participation in government. The revolutionary movements were mainly middle class, except in Sicily, and popular interest and support was generally lacking. Indeed, when a revolution was over, the ordinary people, especially outside the towns, welcomed back their former rulers with open arms. This was largely due to the fact that the liberal, middle-class revolutionaries did not encourage mass involvement in politics. In Italy, as elsewhere in Europe, they feared it would lead to democracy, the replacement of the sovereignty of parliament by the sovereignty of the people, of social stability by social upheaval, of constitutional monarchy by popular republic.

## 4 The Risorgimento

The revolutions of 1820 and 1831, despite their failure, were part of what the Italians call the *Risorgimento* (literally 'resurgence' or 'rebirth'), the movement which led to the formation of a united Italy. Italians do not believe that Italian unification came about suddenly or accidentally as the result of war or diplomacy, but that it was the final stage of their gradual evolution as a nation.

The word *'Risorgimento'* was first used by a dramatist from Piedmont, Vittorio Alfieri, writing at the time of the French Revolution when he made the first clear call of modern times for Italian unity and liberty. Also in the late eighteenth century another Piedmontese, Carlo Denina wrote a history which for the first time dealt with Italy as a whole, not just with Florence, or Naples or Venice. He identified a lack of patriotism among Italians and put it down to the lack of a central government and of a unified legal system '. . . but if there should ever be a war between one of the nations beyond the Alps and Italy, patriotism would certainly rise again.'

The theme of patriotism and national unity was taken up and developed in the 1830s by a young man, Guiseppe Mazzini.

### a) Mazzini

Mazzini was born in 1805 in Genoa. His father was a Professor at the University, and he grew up in an academic and intellectual atmosphere. He was intelligent, sensitive and physically frail, and later in life suffered greatly from depression. His parents, who had wanted him to become a poet, were shocked when he became a revolutionary nationalist. Mazzini himself wrote later that what turned his thoughts to politics was the aftermath of the failed revolution in Piedmont in 1821, when the penniless revolutionaries, passing through Genoa on their way to exile, begged in the streets. He was shocked by their distress, but at the same time inspired by the idea of their devotion to a political cause. He was sixteen, impressionable and an idealist. He began to dress in black, in mourning for the failed revolution, and did so for the rest of his life. He was about to become the archetypal romantic revolutionary.

From 1822 to 1827 he, like so many other young revolutionaries, studied law, and was totally bored by it. He had started to study medicine, but had collapsed at the sight of his first operation. Boredom with the law seemed preferable. The earliest surviving piece of writing by Mazzini was produced at this time '. . . the Fatherland of an Italian is not Rome, Florence or Milan, but the whole of Italy'. He joined the *Carbonari* in 1827 and soon became secretary of the group in Genoa, but found himself dissatisfied with the vagueness of their aims and ambitions.

In November 1830 he was betrayed by one of his fellow *Carbonari* and arrested. He remained in prison for three months and while there he thought out the political ideas which were to dominate the rest of his life. He decided that his life should be dedicated to working for the independence and unification of Italy. This would be done not through the *Carbonari*, whose main interests were driving out the Austrians and forcing the rulers to grant constitutions, but through a new movement 'Young Italy'. Unlike the *Carbonari* it would have clearly defined aims.

His own political philosophy was based on a belief in the existence of God; in the equality of men and of races; in the progress of mankind, and in the rights and duties of the individual in society. His attitude to religion was unusual. He believed that a particular religion could become worn out and that this was now true of Christianity which needed to be replaced by something else. This something else was democracy. God was no longer speaking through priests or the scriptures, but through the People. What the People wanted was therefore the will of God, and as the People wanted national independence and unity this had to be achieved. It would be done through popular risings against their rulers.

* When he was released from prison in 1831 Mazzini settled in Marseilles in the south of France. Here he launched his new secret society, 'Young Italy'.

1   'Young Italy' is a brotherhood of Italians who believe in a law of
     progress and duty, and are convinced that Italy is destined to
     become one nation . . . They join this Association with the firm
     intention of consecrating both thought and action to the great aim
5   of reconstituting Italy as one independent sovereign nation of free
     men and equals.
        'Young Italy' is republican and unitarian – republican because
     theoretically every nation is destined, by the law of God and
     humanity, to form a free and equal community of brothers; and the

10 republican form of government is the only form of government which ensures this future. . . .

'Young Italy' is unitarian, because without unity there is no true nation: because without unity there is no real strength; and Italy, surrounded as she is by powerful, united and jealous nations, has
15 need of strength above all things. . . .
The means by which 'Young Italy' proposes to reach its aim are education and revolution, to be adopted simultaneously and made to harmonize with each other. Education must ever be directed to teach, by example, word and pen, the necessity of revolution.
20 Revolution, whenever it can be realised, must be so conducted as to render it a means of national education. The charcacter of the revolution must be national . . . the flag raised, and the aim proposed, will be national.

Those who joined 'Young Italy' had to swear to dedicate themselves wholly and for ever to the endeavour to make Italy 'one, free, independent republican nation'. Every member had to provide himself with a rifle and fifty rounds of ammunition. The 'ultimate aim' was 'the republic one and indivisible'. Constitutional monarchies were acceptable only as 'governments of transition' on the way to a united republican Italy. There were the usual handshakes and passwords found in all the secret societies: 'What time is it?' – 'Time for the struggle', 'Now – 'and always', and a uniform in national colours: green shirt, red belt, white trousers and a beret.

When Charles Albert finally became King of Piedmont in 1831. Mazzini wrote an open letter to him from Marseilles. He warned him of coming revolution and told him that the people wanted 'liberty, independence and unison. Put yourself at the head of the nation; write on your banner "Union, Liberty, Independence". Free the country from the barbarians. Give your name to a century'. Historians have differed about Mazzini's motives for sending this letter, and about whether his plea was sincere. It is not clear why be wrote the letter at all, for he had little expectation of its success; 'not that I have any hopes in him', he wrote of Charles Albert at the time. In any case why did he, a staunch republican opposed to the monarchy, send this appeal, and what would he have done if Charles Albert had accepted it? There is no evidence available to answer these questions. Perhaps his aim was a negative one – to show that Charles Albert's involvement with liberalism ten years before was now over, that nationalists could not therefore expect any help from the monarchy and that their only hope lay with the republicans.

The next two years were spent organizing 'Young Italy'. Originally the upper age limit for members was 40, but it was afterwards raised to include a few older men. Propaganda materials were distributed throughout Piedmont, Tuscany and the Papal States. The first Mazzinian revolt took place in Piedmont among the army, but was betrayed and the conspiracy savagely crushed by the government. Other Mazzinian revolutionary adventures, however serious in intention, too often degenerated into farce. This series of events of 1833 reads like the scenario of a comic opera: for a planned attack on Piedmont, through Savoy, Mazzini began to collect volunteers in Switzerland among Polish, German and Italian refugees. The military command was given to General Ramorino from Genoa, and Mazzini gave him money to raise and organize an army. Ramorino took the money to Paris, where he lost it gambling, and returned to Mazzini without an army and without the money. All Mazzini had to depend on were the few hundred men he himself had collected. Just before they were ready to leave for Piedmont, the Swiss authorities surrounded and disbanded the Polish and German volunteers. This left less than two hundred men, and Ramorino felt there was no point in going on with so few. He gave orders for them to disperse. Mazzini disagreed, and while the two men argued, the soldiers obeyed their commander's orders and went home. The expedition ended before it began.

In 1833 a chance meeting with Mazzini in Marseilles led to a young man joining 'Young Italy', and involving himself in a proposed rising in Genoa. The scheme failed and he was sentenced to death, but fortunately for Italy he had escaped before the trial and sentence was passed in his absence. The young man was Guiseppe Garibaldi, later to be one of the great figures in the story of Italian unification.

The Mazzinian dream was not realized in the years 1833–34. Its basis was too intellectual and too idealistic to be a practical or popular blueprint for revolution. Mazzini remained in exile until 1848 but kept in touch with events in Italy and continued his political activities from a distance.

How great was his influence in the 1830s and 1840s? His writings, most of which read like vague mysticism, had only a limited circulation in his lifetime. Well received, if not well understood by intellectual revolutionaries, his books and pamphlets did not contain much of general interest. Most of his earlier writings sold only a few hundred copies each. Mazzini has been blamed by Marxist historians for failure to realize the needs of the peasants and for not working for agrarian reform. This, they argue, would have won him widespread support and turned his movement into a popular one. He himself estimated the membership of 'Young Italy' at about 50 000, but most historians think this is probably an overestimate. The revolutionary attacks, demonstrations and mutinies which he inspired all ended more or less ignominiously with nothing practical achieved.

Yet his name was known throughout Italy. The quiet, gentle man whose recreations were playing the guitar and smoking cigars, who spent years in impoverished exile in London, earned respect, admiration and even devotion from all who met him. His great strength was to inspire in others the same enthusiasm for and dedication to the cause of Italian

unity that he had himself.
* The nationalist movement of the 1840s was weak. This was mainly due to the diversity of opinion within it about the form which a united Italy should take. While Mazzini and his extremist supporters preached revolution and extolled the virtues of a democratic republic as the only true ideal, other proposals were being put forward. Books published in Piedmont indicate that moderate nationalists there supported a different approach. They favoured the idea of Piedmont leading the Italian States in a bid to evict the Austrians and argued that only Piedmont had the strength and resources to fight Austria. There could be no independent united Italy while the Austrians still controlled Lombardy and Venetia. Therefore, all the other states should accept the predominance of Piedmont and rally round in support. It was only a short step for more extreme monarchists to begin canvassing for Charles Albert to be considered as the future king of a united Italy.

b) Pius IX

There was, however, another contender for leadership. Another Pied-montese, Gioberti, published a book called *Of the Moral and Civil Primacy of the Italians* in 1843. Much of it was political fantasy, worthy of Mazzini at his most impractical, but it did contain a new idea. He thought, that as the Pope and the Catholic Church were the glories of Italy, they should play an important part in its national revival. The Italian states should form themselves into a federation under the Presidency of the Pope. Five thousand copies of Gioberti's book were quickly sold, but the reputation of the government of the Papal States as oppressive and corrupt was a stumbling block to his proposals being put into practice.

The situation was changed by the election in 1846 of a new Pope, Puis IX, who was known to have liberal sympathies. He had been born into a noble family in 1792. His parents intended him for a military career but poor health (he was certainly very highly strung and may even have suffered from epilepsy) prevented this, and he turned to the Church. He was made a Cardinal in 1839. His election as Pope was unexpected for it had been thought that Metternich would engineer the election of a conservative-minded Cardinal. The election of Puis IX was even more surprising for he was not even the favourite candidate among the liberal Cardinals.

His period as Pope, from 1846 to 1878, was one of the longest and most momentous. It began with a grand gesture to the liberals when he granted an amnesty to all political prisoners. As a result two thousand men most of them revolutionaries, were freed. Work began on reforms in administration, education and the law, and laymen were given a larger part in public affairs. In 1847 he ended censorship of the press, and by the end of the year over a hundred independent newspapers were circulating in the Papal States. Some of these were openly revolutionary, giving detailed information about meetings and demonstrations. Political clubs were established in the towns, and membership grew quickly. In Rome a civic guard was formed. The Pope intended that it should protect property and prevent violence, but it soon showed every sign of becoming an organization of the people and beyond the control of the Papal authorities. Another important development of 1847 was the Pope's decision to create the *Consulta*. This was an advisory body, similar to other bodies which already existed to advise the Pope, but with two important differences: it was elected, not appointed, and it included members of the laity among its representatives.

The reform in the Papal States set an example for others to follow. In Piedmont and Tuscany the press was freed by the end of 1847, and proposals were made for a joint custom union between the two states and the Papal States. Agitation for reform spread, even into Austrian-controlled Lombardy, causing Metternich grave concern. He acted to preserve Austrian authority by making new treaties with Modena and Parma and by extending the Austrian garrison of the castle of Ferrara to cover the whole town which lay on the Papal side of the border with Lombardy. This brought a sharp protest from the Pope, and Metternich was obliged to withdraw the troops back into the castle.

## 5 The Revolutions of 1848–9

The general discontent in Italy, the demands of the liberals for constitutions, for administrative reforms and political freedoms in the individual states, and the demands of the nationalists for Italian unity and independence from Austria, were bound up with a wider economic crisis covering all Europe in 1848.

About 90 per cent of the population of Italy worked on the land and the economy was based almost entirely on agriculture. There was very little industry anywhere, and in the south almost none at all. Harvest failures like those of 1846 and 1847 were disastrous, especially for the peasants. Shortages of wheat and maize meant high prices, and as wages did not rise to meet the increased costs, those peasants earning day wages could not afford to feed their families. Peasants who worked for the landowner in return for a small piece of land were equally badly off when the harvest failed. People in the towns, where food was also scarce and dear, suffered too. Revolutions broke out.

* They began in Sicily where Ferdinand II, who became King of Naples in 1830, had at first offered a better life for Sicilians by instituting reforms and appointing a viceroy to take charge of the island and ensure that the reforms were carried out. This state of affairs had not lasted, and an era of repression coinciding with an outbreak of cholera had left the Sicilians in a desperate state.

In January 1848 notices were circulated in Palermo:

1  Sicilians! the time for prayers is passed; peaceful protests and
   demonstrations, all have been useless. Ferdinand, King of Naples,
   has treated them all with contempt, and we, as people born free,
   are loaded with chains and reduced to misery. Shall we still delay
5  claiming our lawful rights? To arms, sons of Sicily; our united
   force will be invincible. . . . Heaven will not fail to support our
   just undertaking. Sicilians, to arms!

The notice went on to explain how people were to obtain arms. They
would be handed out to those who came to the main piazza at dawn three
days later (although in fact the organizers had not made proper
arrangements for getting arms, and only a few weapons were available).
The authorities could not really believe in a revolution announced in
advance, but they took no chances and arrested a few likely suspects.
   Early on the day announced the streets were full of people, but there is
no evidence to show whether they were revolutionaries or mere
sightseers. After what arms were available had been handed out, there
were clashes between the people and the troops, and the next day
peasants from outside the city arrived to join in the rising. The
Neapolitan army replied by shelling the city and two days later
reinforcements of 5000 troops arrived from Naples. They found that the
revolutionaries had taken over the city and were demanding a restoration of the famous 1812 constitution which the King of Naples had
abolished in 1816. The King offered a compromise, which was refused.
   Fighting continued, and by April the revolutionaries had taken over
most of the island. A provisional government was set up by upper- and
middle-class moderates who had become anxious about the activities of
their peasant associates. A national civic guard was formed 'to control
the masses', who were marching on towns and villages, burning tax
collection records, destroying property and freeing prisoners. In March
an elected Parliament met and declared that Naples and Sicily were
finally and totally separated and divided, and that the King of Naples
was no longer King of Sicily. The Sicilians' aim in 1848, as in 1820, was
to gain independence from Naples; theirs was a separatist movement,
not a movement concerned with the idea of national unity.
   * On the mainland the revolution spread to Naples within a few days
of the uprising in Palermo. A huge demonstration in the city of Naples
demanded a constitution. The King agreed to a two-chamber parliament
with limited power. He also agreed to form a national guard and to free
the press from censorship. But peasant discontent over changes affecting
their right to use common land led to an outbreak of fighting. The King
was able to use this as an excuse to appoint a right wing government in
May. The rising was suppressed and by September the government was
able to send troops to retake Sicily. The Sicilians were defeated and were
forced in the spring of 1849 to accept reunification with Naples. There
the King had already gone back on his promises, abolished the

parliament and replaced it with absolute rule and a police state.

* Elsewhere in Italy serious disturbances broke out in 1848. As a result the Grand Duke of Tuscany and the King of Piedmont promised constitutions in February and the Pope followed their example in March, while the rulers of Modena and Parma had to leave their Duchies. Early in the year trouble started in Milan, in Austrian-controlled Lombardy. This revolution, like that in Sicily, was different from the revolutions in the rest of Italy, for it too was a rising against an occupying power. It began as a tobacco boycott. Tobacco was an Austrian state monopoly and the people of Milan believed that if they stopped smoking, Austrian revenues would be seriously affected. The sight of Austrian soldiers smoking in the streets was an excuse for the Milanese to show their dislike of the troops, and small scale fights broke out, quickly followed by larger riots and eventually by a full scale revolution during 'The Five Days' of 17–22 March. The Austrian commander, 81-year-old General Radetzky, decided to withdraw from the city, for a few days earlier the situation in Austria had changed dramatically. Revolution had broken out in Vienna, and Metternich had been dismissed.

The provisional government set up in Milan by the revolutionaries prepared to continue the fight against Austria and turned for help to Charles Albert, King of Piedmont, who had just granted a constitution to his people. After a week of indecision, Charles Albert was persuaded to declare war on Austria and the provisional government in Milan issued an emotional and inaccurate proclamation to their fellow citizens.

1   We have conquered. We have compelled the enemy to fly, oppressed as much by his own shame as our valour; but scattered in our fields, wandering like wild beasts, united in bands of plunderers, he prolongs for us the horrors of war without affording
5   any of its sublime emotions. This makes it easy to understand that the arms we have taken up, and still hold, can never be laid down as long as one of his band shall be hid under cover of the Alps. We have sworn, we swear it again, with the generous Prince who flies to associate himself with our glory – all Italy swears it, and so it shall
10   be.
To arms then, to arms, to secure the fruits of our glorious revolution – to fight the last battle of independence and the Italian Union.

Events were moving at the same time in the other Austrian controlled state, Venetia. A small scale rising persuaded the Austrian authorities to surrender, and the Independent Venetian Republic of St Mark was proclaimed on 22 March. Its rapidly elected assembly voted for union with Piedmont.

* At first things went well for Charles Albert and his army defeated the Austrians at the end of May. But in the Papal States events were causing concern. The Pope's military commander had disobeyed orders and had

set off with his troops to join Charles Albert's army. This put the Pope, who was not at war with Austria, in a difficult position. He decided to dissociate himself from the war, and in the Allocution, an official policy speech made to Church dignitaries he made his position clear.

1  . . . But, seeing that some at present desire that We too, along with the other Princes of Italy and their subjects, should engage in war against the Austrians, We have thought it convenient to proclaim clearly and openly in this our solemn Assembly, that such a
5  measure is altogether alien from our counsels, inasmuch as We, albeit unworthy, are upon earth the viceregent of Him that is the Author of Peace and Lover of Charity, and, conformably to the function of our supreme Apostolate, We reach to and embrace all kindreds, peoples, and nations, with equal solicitude of paternal
10  affection. But if, notwithstanding, there are not wanting among our subjects those who allow themselves to be carried away by the example of the rest of the Italians, in what manner could We possibly curb their ardour?

And in this place We cannot refrain from repudiating, before the
15  face of all nations, the treacherous advice, published moreover in journals, and in various works, of those who would have the Roman Pontiff to be the head and to preside over the formation of some sort of novel Republic of the whole Italian people. Rather, on this occasion, moved hereto by the love We bear them, We do
20  urgently warn and exhort the said Italian people to abstain with all diligence from the like counsels, deceitful and ruinous to Italy herself, and to abide in close attachment to their respective Sovereigns, of whose good-will they have already had experience, so as never to let themselves be torn away from the obedience they
25  owe them. For if they should do otherwise, they not only would fail in their own duty, but would also run a risk of rending Italy herself, every day more and more, with fresh discords and intestine factions.

The Allocution not only made it clear that the Pope would not fight against Austria, but also that he was drawing back from the idea that he should head an Italian federation, and even from the idea of the Church's support of a united Italy. The Pope, who had two years earlier, 'blessed "Italy" ', had withdrawn the blessing. The Church had turned her back on liberalism and gone over to the side of reaction and absolutism. For Charles Albert and other loyal Catholics the loss of Papal support for their cause was a bitter blow. They had to choose between following their political principles and obeying their spiritual leader. Many chose the former course and as a result the liberal and nationalist movements became markedly anti-clerical, especially among the extremists.

When General Radetzky withdrew from Milan his army took refuge in the Quadrilateral, four virtually impregnable fortresses, and waited

*Pope Pius IX, cartoon of 1852*

there for reinforcements from Austria. These had arrived by the end of June and in July Charles Albert's army was defeated by the Austrians at Custozza. An armistice was signed and Piedmont withdrew from Lombardy, leaving it in Austrian hands. The Venetians hurriedly renounced their recently completed union with Piedmont, re-established the Republic of St Mark and prepared to continue the war with Austria.
\* At this point Mazzini arrived back in Italy. The 'war of the Princes' against Austria had failed; now it was time for the 'war of the People'.

In Rome the murder of the Pope's unpopular chief minister at the end of November was followed by rioting. The Pope fled from the disturbed city and took refuge in Naples, while the government which he had left behind announced a programme of reform. They abolished the hated tax on grinding corn, provided public building work for the unemployed and proposed the holding of a *Costituente*, a meeting in Rome of representatives from all parts of Italy. The election of these representatives was organized by a special 'Junta of State' chosen by the government of Rome and the *Costituente* met for the first time in February 1849. One of its members was Garibaldi. Four days later the *Costituente* proclaimed the overthrow of the temporal power of the Pope and the establishment of the Republic.

In March Mazzini arrived in Rome, to be elected as head of the Triumvirate, a group of three men who were to rule the city. This they did in a fair, tolerant and enlightened way for the remaining months of the Republic's life. The Pope appealed to France, Spain and Naples to help free Rome from 'the enemies of our most holy religion and civil society', and an army of about 20 000 men was sent by the French Republic to destroy the Roman Republic. The gallant defence of the city by Garibaldi became one of the legends of the *Risorgimento* but the odds were too great and the city fell at the end of June 1849.

Why did the Roman Republic fight so fiercely? Mazzini gave his answer:

1  To the many other causes which decided us to resist, there was one
   intimately bound up with the aim of my whole life – the foundation
   of an national unity. Rome was the natural centre of that unity, and
   it was important to attract the eyes and reverence of my
5  countrymen towards her. . . . It was essential to redeem Rome; to
   place her once again at the summit so that the Italians might again
   learn to regard her as the temple of their common country. . . . I
   had faith in her. . . . The defence of the city was therefore decided
   upon; by the assembly and people of Rome from a noble impulse
10 and from reverence for the honour of Italy; by me as the logical
   consequence of a long-matured design.

After the fall of the city he appealed to the citizens:

1  Romans, your city has been overcome by brute force, but your

rights are neither lessened nor changed. By all you hold sacred, citizens, keep yourselves uncontaminated. Organize peaceful demonstrations. Let your municipalities unceasingly declare with
5 calm firmness that they voluntarily adhere to the Republican form of government and the abolition of the temporal Power of the Pope; and that they regard as illegal whatever government be imposed without the free approval of the people. . . . In the streets, the theatres, in every place of meeting let the same cry be heard. . . .
10 Thousands cannot be imprisoned. Men cannot be compelled to degrade themselves.

The Pope returned to Rome in the afternoon of 12th April 1850, and ·vas cheered through the streets by the same citizens who had cheered for Mazzini, Garibaldi and the Roman Republic a year earlier, clear evidence that for most ordinary people the ending of the hardships they had endured in the past months was preferable to the hope of liberty and national unity.

* In Venetia, the other Italian Republic had held out courageously against a siege by the Austrian navy. The city was heavily shelled during May and June 1849 and a severe outbreak of cholera added to the miseries of starving Venetians. The city finally surrendered to the Austrians in August 1849.

* Meanwhile Charles Albert had re-entered the war against Austria in March 1849 when he denounced the armistice with Austria. His reasons for doing so are uncertain. Was he driven to it, as some historians have suggested, by haunting memories of the battle of Custozza and horror at the subsequent sufferings of Lombardy abandoned to the Austrians? Or was he personally smarting under the humiliation of defeat and the failure of his cause? Or perhaps, after six months, he had simply had enough time to regroup his forces and was ready for action to avenge the past. It appears also that he was misled into believing that France would come to his support if he re-entered the war. Vengeance was not to be his, for in April he was heavily defeated at the battle of Novara. His spirit finally broken he abdicated in favour of his son, Victor Emmanuel II.

* In Tuscany the Grand Duke had granted a constitution at the beginning of 1848. When news of the March revolution in Vienna and the fall of Metternich reached Tuscany the government decided to send a small army to fight the Austrians. Workers in the cities began to agitate about pay and conditions, and middle-class radicals began to preach republicanism. In January 1849 the Grand Duke could stand it no longer and left for that haven of absolutism, Naples. A revolutionary provisional government was set up and a dictator was appointed as a prelude to establishing a republic. But before this could be done, Charles Albert was defeated at Novara. This left the Austrian army free to move into Tuscany, where they crushed the revolution and restored the Grand Duke to his throne. In Modena and Parma the rulers, who had fled

during the revolutions, were also restored by Austrian military power.

## 6 Failure of the Revolutions of 1848–9

By the middle of 1849 it was clear that the revolutions had failed, just as they had failed in 1820 and 1831. In Sicily Neapolitan rule had been re-established and the Two Sicilies forcibly reunited under a more absolute and repressive regime than before. In the Papal States the Roman Republic had been destroyed, the Pope restored to temporal power by foreign soldiers who occupied Rome, and liberal hopes of Papal support for national unity shattered. Venetia and Lombardy had failed in their bid for independence from Austria and remained as firmly under Austrian control as ever, while the rulers of Tuscany, Modena and Parma had been restored by Austrian military intervention. Piedmont had been defeated by the Austrians.

Apart from the *Statuto*, granted to Piedmont by Charles Albert, none of the constitutions obtained from their rulers by the revolutionaries had survived. None of the States which gained independence – Sicily, Lombardy and Venetia – had retained it, and none of the rulers forced out of their states had been kept out for long.

*  The revolutions had been an almost total failure. There were a number of different reasons for this. There was a general lack of co-operation between revolutionary groups. Sicily and Naples were an extreme case of mutual hostility, but elsewhere there was little inter-state help or support. In Piedmont the King would not accept volunteers from other states in his army nor work with any other revolutionary groups unless they first declared their loyalty to the Piedmontese royal family. There was no concerted effort despite the fact that, apart from those in Sicily, the revolutionaries had two main aims in common.

The belief was still current among liberals that Italian nationalism could only develop after constitutional government had been established in all the states. This belief was disputed by the radicals, whose policies were republican, but constitutional government remained the first priority of the moderate majority of the revolutionaries. While they might have been divided on domestic politics, liberals and radicals were united in the second aim, to expel the foreigner, Austria, and found a united and independent Italy.

This programme might have worked if there had been a single national leader to co-ordinate policy. There were at least three possible candidates, Mazzini, Pius IX and Charles Albert, none of whom for different reasons achieved the leadership, and each of whom had a different political philosophy. This confusion of ideologies is reflected in the different provisional revolutionary governments which were set up, which were moderate, extremist, liberal, republican, democratic or monarchist in varying combinations.

In the end it was not just lack of co-ordination which led to the failure of the revolutions. The provisional governments were inexperienced, weak and lacking in resources, particularly military ones. They could not maintain themselves in power once they had achieved it. This was partly due to lack of popular support by the masses, except at the height of the revolution. Popular involvement was not encouraged by the liberals as politics was thought to be largely a middle-class pre-occupation. In most cases peasants found little or no improvement in their lives under a liberal revolutionary government. Social reform was not a liberal platform. As a result rulers who had been dispossessed were welcomed back quite sincerely by the ordinary people. Where republics were successfully established by radicals, as in Rome and Venetia, they were destroyed by the military power of France or Austria.

The military superiority of Austria was probably the single most important factor in the failure of the revolutions. The Austrian armies were superior in numbers, as well as being better equipped and much better led than any other army in the peninsula. In any conflict they were bound to win in the end, even against combined revolutionary forces. It was by Austrian military intervention and with Austrian support that the old regimes were restored in 1849.

The lesson of the 1848–9 revolutions was that Austria held the key to Italian unity and had no intention of unlocking the door. But the situation was soon to change in one important respect. During the 1850s in Piedmont, where the *Statuto* remained in force, there were opportunities for political life to continue in a way which was not possible elsewhere in the peninsula. Refugees from other Italian states settled in Piedmont, more than 200 000 of them in Turin and Genoa. They gave Piedmont a cosmopolitan nationalist flavour which was new.

The dominant political personality during the 1850s was the nobleman Count Camillo Benso di Cavour, a great, some would say the greatest, figure in the history of the unification of Italy.

---

**Making notes on 'Italy 1815–1852'**

Your notes on Italy in the years 1815 to 1852 should be aimed at helping you to understand the development of liberalism and nationalism during this period of Austrian domination. They should also give you an understanding of the revolutions of 1820, 1831, and 1848–49 and why they failed.

The following headings and sub-headings should help you:

1.   The Italian States
1.1.   The Napoleonic background
1.2.   The Vienna Settlement
1.3.   Liberals
1.4.   Radicals

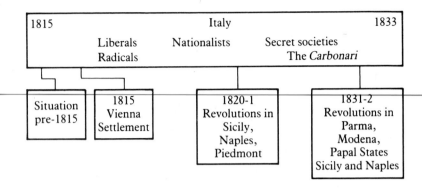

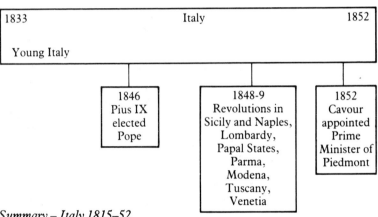

*Summary – Italy 1815–52*

1.5. Nationalists
1.6. The 'Restored regimes' in
   The Papal States
   Piedmont
   Sicily
1.7. The Secret Societies
   The *Carbonari*
2.   The Revolutions of 1820
2.1. Naples
2.2. Sicily
2.3. Metternich's system
2.4. Piedmont
3.   The Revolutions of 1831
3.1. Modena, Parma and the Papal States
3.2. Why did the revolutions fail in 1820–1 and 1831–2?

---

### Answering essay questions on 'Italy 1815–52'

You are unlikely to be given an opportunity to answer an essay question that is totally restricted to this period. But you will be expected to use evidence from this period in a more general essay. Examples of such questions are given on pages 3–4 and pages 92–3.

You will need to have arguments clearly in your mind to explain the reasons for the failure of the revolutions of 1820, 1831 and 1848. Some of the possible explanations apply equally to all the revolutions. Some are specific to a particular place or a particular time.

Make a list of the revolutions/uprisings that took place in Italy between 1820 and 1849. For each one indicate which of the following help to explain its failure: poor leadership; disunity; lack of popular support; unrealistic aims; lack of military strength; government action; foreign intervention.

You should now be in a good position to decide what points you would wish to make in answering the question, 'Why did the revolutions in Italy between 1820 and 1849 all fail to achieve their objectives?' Prepare an essay plan for this question. Your plan should be made up of between three and five major points, with an indication of the evidence you would include to support each one.

## Source-based questions on 'Italy 1815–1852'

**1 The annexation of Genoa by Piedmont**
Read carefully the extract from the letter written by the Piedmontese ambassador, given on page 9. Answer the following questions:
a) What three problems does the ambassador see in the annexation of Genoa by Piedmont?
b) What is the ambassador's stated view on the possibility of successfully mixing the people of Piedmont and Genoa? What does his honest point of view appear to be? Explain your answer.
c) Compose a short general statement about one of the problems facing those who supported Italian unification in the early nineteenth century, which the evidence in this extract would support.

**2 Mazzini's 'Young Italy'**
Read carefully the extract from Mazzini's statement about 'Young Italy', given on page 16. Answer the following questions:
a) What were the aims of the 'Young Italy' society? Illustrate your answer with a quotation from the source.
b) What is the meaning of 'a law of progress and duty' (lines 1–2)?
c) What methods did Mazzini intend 'Young Italy' to use to achieve its aims?
d) How could Mazzini's statement about methods be used to support the argument that he was an intellectual idealist rather than a practical politician?
e) Identify two assumptions that Mazzini makes in his statement. For each, comment on the validity of the assumption. Provide evidence to support your view.

**3 Calls to arms in Sicily and Milan**
Read carefully the extracts from the calls to arms issued in Sicily and Milan in 1848, given on pages 21 and 22. Answer the following questions:
a) Summarize in one sentence the *rational* argument used in the Sicilian call to arms.
b) Its appeal is also to the *emotions*. What emotions are being appealed to? Support your answer with evidence.
c) The Milanese proclamation also appeals to the *emotions*. What emotions are being appealed to? Support your answer with evidence.
d) Both extracts offer evidence to the student of 'The Unification of Italy'. Write a short paragraph showing how each extract illuminates differing opinions about unification in Italy in 1848.
e) How far are the factual statements made within the extracts to be relied upon? Explain your answer.

**4 Pius IX's change of policy**
Read carefully the extract from Pius IX's 'Allocution' of 1848, given
on page 23, and study the cartoon of 1852, reproduced on page 24.
Answer the following questions:
a) Summarize the argument used by Pius IX to justify his decision
not to engage in war against the Austrians in 1848.
b) What is the meaning of the final sentence of the first paragraph of
the 'Allocution'?
c) What is the political point of view put forward by the artist of the
cartoon? Support your answer with evidence.
d) Quote evidence from the 'Allocution' to support the view of Pius
IX put forward by the artist of the cartoon. Explain your answer.

**5 Mazzini and the Roman Republic, 1849**
Read carefully Mazzini's explanation of the decision to fight so fiercely
to defend the Roman Republic, and his appeal to the people of Rome,
given on pages 25–6. Answer the following questions:
a) Summarize Mazzini's explanation of the Roman Republic's decision to resist.
b) Is Mazzini's explanation convincing? Support your answer with
evidence.
c) In his appeal to the people of Rome, what action is Mazzini asking
to be avoided and to be taken?
d) In what ways do these extracts from sources support the argument
you put forward in answer to 2 d) above?
e) Mazzini's appeal had little effect. Write a short paragraph
explaining *general reasons* why this might have been so.

# CHAPTER 2

# Piedmont, Cavour and Italy

## 1 Piedmont

\* In 1720 the Dukes of Savoy, who ruled over the poor and backward peasant state of Piedmont in north west Italy, acquired the island of Sardinia and with it the title of king. The combined state, properly known as the Kingdom of Sardinia, was sometimes called Sardinia – Piedmont, but more usually just Piedmont.

At the end of the eighteenth century Piedmont was sparsely populated, for although the birth rate was high, the death rate was higher and life expectancy was short. Turin, the capital, had a declining population, there was little or no industry and the countryside was economically undeveloped. But Piedmont had a strong army and an efficient administration. It also had absolute monarchy.

At the beginning of the Napoleonic wars, Piedmont became an ally of Austria. The Piedmontese royal family was closely united by marriage with the French royal family and this was enough to make Piedmont a natural enemy of the French Republic. An attack on Savoy and Nice in the western part of Piedmont by the French army in 1792 sealed the union of Piedmont and Austria in the fight against France. The war turned out badly for Piedmont which during 1799, and again from 1802 to 1814 was annexed to France. This brought Piedmont directly into contact with French law and administration. Piedmontese schools were merged into the French system and Piedmontese youths were conscripted into the French army. French was the language of polite society, which became increasingly French in custom and thought. There was little concerted opposition to French rule. The middle classes even found some advantages in the new system, such as career opportunities in government service and the army previously open only to the nobility. Only towards the end of the Napoleonic era in Italy did anti-French secret societies arise in Piedmont.

In 1814, after the defeat of Napoleon, the King of Piedmont, Victor Emmanuel I returned to Turin to 'the good and faithful subjects who would find themselves once more under the dominion of these beloved Princes, who had brought them happiness and glory for so many centuries.' To sweeten his reception, Victor Emmanuel abolished conscription and reduced taxation but these were his only concessions. On the advice of his ministers, men of the pre-war regime, he issued a royal edict proclaiming that the legal constitution of Piedmont was contained in laws made before 1800, and that these could not be changed. Piedmont once again became an absolute monarchy. The French legal system, the Code Napoléon, was repealed, equality before the law was abolished, and free and open criminal trials became things of the past. As a gesture of goodwill, however, torture was not reintroduced.

* The Vienna Settlement gave Piedmont control of the former Republic of Genoa. This was of great benefit to Piedmont, for the city of Genoa was an important port. The Genoese were not enthusiastic. They resented the loss of their former independence, first to France during the Napoleonic annexation, and then to Piedmont. The Congress of Vienna tried to soften the blow by laying down conditions for the administration of Genoa by Piedmont, including the election of provincial councils and the imposition of no more than reasonable taxation. But these conditions were difficult to enforce, and Genoa suffered from commercial restrictions imposed by Piedmont which hampered trade.

## a) Charles Albert

In 1819 modernization of the administration of Piedmont began, but this was quickly discontinued in the alarms of the revolutions of 1820. Afterwards membership of secret revolutionary societies in Piemont increased, and a growing number of liberals began to hope for some sort of reforming initiative from the monarchy. There was little chance of such action from Victor Emmanuel I, or from his brother and heir presumptive, but the second in line to the throne, Charles Albert, gave more hope to the liberals.

Charles Albert was a strange, reserved young man, who had been brought up in exile in France. On his return to Piedmont he saw just how archaic and repressive Victor Emmanuel's government was. He showed sympathy with revolutionary students injured in riots in Turin in 1821 and was known to have contacts with revolutionary officers in the army. In March 1821 the liberals appealed to him to lead a revolution. It appears that he agreed to do so, although he later denied it. Perhaps he did intend to lead the revolution and only denied it when the revolution failed. It has also been suggested, although there is no clear evidence for it, that perhaps he was acting as a government agent and only pretending to be in sympathy with the revolutionaries in order to obtain information about their activities. Such action would be in keeping with his secretive and devious character. Perhaps, and probably most likely, he really had not made up his mind and was just dithering. At any rate, so began 'the legend of Charles Albert'.

While he was hesitating, a revolutionary committee seized the fortress of Alessandria in Genoa, established a provisional government calling itself 'The Kingdom of Italy' and declared war on Austria. Pressure on Victor Emmanuel to grant liberal reforms grew. He refused, but hearing of a second army mutiny, this time at Turin, he decided to abdicate and left for Nice, close to the western frontier of Piedmont, while revolution spread through his kingdom (see page 13).

His brother and heir, Charles Felix, who eventually succeeded him, died in 1831 and Charles Albert finally became King of Piedmont. Since 1815 the government had been conspicuously unenlightened and dominated by the Church, and it looked as if it would continue unaltered. Despite his flirtation with the rebels in 1821, Charles Albert began his reign as a reactionary, signing an alliance with Austria and threatening to attack the French liberal government. Yet in 1848–9 Piedmont was to fight Austria in support of a liberal revolution in Austrian-controlled Lombardy, and Charles Albert was to grant his people a constitution, which would be the basis of the constitutional monarchy of a united Italy twenty years later.

* Historians have tried to find explanations for this change in Charles Albert from reactionary to liberal nationalist without much success. One suggestion is that he had been all his life a nationalist or even a secret revolutionary, and once he became king was merely waiting for an opportunity to declare himself. This however does not seem very convincing. More probably the answer lies in the inconsistencies and uncertainties of his complex personality.

His whole career was one of contradictions. He seems to have been secretive and unsociable, a typical introvert, and he seldom showed any emotion. He was excessively devout, wore a hairshirt, and was much attracted to the more mystical aspects of the Catholic Church. He was liable to self deception, and believed for instance, without any foundation in fact, that he was cut out to be a soldier and leader of men. He could be energetic and enterprising on a short-term basis, but lacked the determination to carry things through. More important, his view of life was entirely divorced from reality.

* His policies in the early years of his reign illustrate the uncertainty of his political beliefs. On the one hand he refused to pardon political prisoners left over from the 1821 revolutions and increased still further the influence of the Church in Piedmont. He extended the already severe censorship, and as a result, Mazzini and Garibaldi left Piedmont in a hurry, soon to be followed by Gioberti, the spokesman for liberal Catholics. Gioberti, who was unable to publish his proposals for an Italian federation under the Presidency of the Pope because of the censorship laws in Piedmont, emigrated to the more liberal climate of Brussels. Other Piedmontese liberals, including Cavour, left Piedmont, that 'intellectual hell', preferring to live in the greater freedom found almost anywhere else, including Austrian Lombardy.

On the other hand some of Charles Albert's early actions were those of a reformer. He made a number of beneficial changes in trade laws, reduced tariffs and signed trade treaties with other states. He clarified the legal code, and allowed non-nobles to fill senior posts in the army and on the royal council.

During the 1840s liberalising influences from other parts of Italy crept into Piedmont. In 1841 social, non-political groups were allowed to meet freely for the first time. These groups were unimportant in themselves but significant in that they were permitted to exist at all. It was a small step towards a more liberal regime. Piedmont also hosted several scientific congresses. These all-Italian congresses played an important part in spreading nationalist ideas, and at one held in 1846 in Piedmont a speaker referred to Charles Albert as the Italian leader who would drive out the foreigners. From this time at least he seems to have thought of himself in this capacity, if only in a theoretical way and without any practical expectation.

* As the 1840s went by pressure for liberal reforms increased. In Turin demands for a constitution came from the small but articulate middle and professional classes. In Genoa, where the influence of Mazzini was strong, the demands were more violent and more radical, not just for a constitution but for renewal of the former republic. Unrest spread to Turin and noisy demonstrations in October 1847 and the threat of revolution persuaded Charles Albert to agree to make reforms and to grant a constitution early in 1848. As a devout Catholic he was probably influenced by the limited constitutional reforms which the Pope had introduced in the Papal States.

Charles Albert's general reforms were largely limited to taking some power out of the hands of the monarchy and putting it into those of the bureaucracy. For instance, the police were now to be under the control of a minister of the interior. Local government was also organized and local councils elected.

* The constitution was issued in the form of 14 articles, on 8 February, 1848, and known as the *Statuto*.

1 . . . 'Now, therefore, that the times are ripe for greater things, and, in the midst of the changes which have occurred in Italy, we hesitate no longer to give our people the most solemn proof that we are able to give of the faith which we continue to repose in their
5 devotion and discretion. . . .
. . . for the present we have much pleasure in declaring that, with the advice and approval of our Ministers and the principal advisers of our Crown, we have resolved and determined to adopt the following bases of a fundamental statute for the establishment
10 in our states of a complete system of representative Government.
*Article 1*. The Catholic, apostolic, and Roman religion is the sole religion of the state.
The other forms of public worship at present existing are tolerated in conformity with the laws.
15 *Article 2*. The person of the Sovereign is sacred and inviolable. His ministers are responsible.
*Article 3*. To the King alone appertains the executive power. He is the supreme head of the State. He commands all the forces, both naval and military; declares war, concludes treaties of peace,
20 alliance, and commerce; nominates to all offices, and gives all the necessary orders for the execution of the laws without suspending or dispensing with the observance thereof.

*Article 4.* The King alone sanctions and promulgates the laws.
*Article 5.* All justice emanates from the King, and is administered
25 in his name. He may grant mercy and commute punishment.
*Article 6.* The legislative power will be collectively exercised by the
King and by two Chambers.
*Article 7.* The first of these Chambers will be composed of Members
nominated by the King for life; the second will be elective, on the
30 basis of the census to be determined.
*Article 8.* The proposal of laws will appertain to the King and to
each of the Chambers, but with the distinct understanding that all
laws imposing taxes must originate in the elective Chamber.
*Article 9.* The King convokes the two Chambers annually,
35 prorogues their sessions, and may dissolve the elective one; but in
this case he will convoke a new assembly at the expiration of four
months.
*Article 10.* No tax may be imposed or levied if not assented to by the
Chambers and sanctioned by the King.
40 *Article 11.* The press will be free, but subject to restraining laws.
*Article 12.* Individual liberty will be guaranteed.
*Article 13.* The judges, . . . will be irremovable, after having
exercised their functions for a certain space of time, to be hereafter
determined.
45 *Article 14.* We reserve to ourselves the power of establishing a
district militia . . . composed of persons who may pay a rate, which
will be fixed upon hereafter. This militia will be placed under the
command of the administrative authority, and in dependence on
the Minister of the Interior.
50 The King will have the power of suspending or dissolving it in
places where he may deem it opportune so to do.' . . .

These articles were not very clearly expressed and some historians
believe that this was intentional and was a way for Charles Albert to keep
his options open. Phrases like 'The King's ministers are responsible' left
doubts as to whom or for what they were responsible – to the King? to
parliament? very little was clearly defined – what exactly were the
'restraining laws' limiting the freedom of the press, for instance?
    The full *Statuto* was published in March 1848. It included a number of
other clauses providing for equality before the law for all, regardless of
religion (although Catholicism remained the state religion), and for equal
employment opportunities for all. It did not decide who was going to
have the vote to elect the Lower Chamber. This was fixed later, on a
literacy and taxpaying franchise, giving the vote to about two per cent of
the population. The constitution was not a Parliamentary one except in a
very limited way, because the King retained most of his existing rights.
Nevertheless it was too radical for Charles Albert's ministers and they
were replaced by moderate liberal nationalists.

Charles Albert's motives for granting the constitution are not clear. Was he sincere, or merely acting from fear of a revolution? Was it a sudden change of heart, or was he merely bringing out into the open his real sympathies previously kept hidden? Or was it just another example of his inconsistent behaviour? Historians continue to argue the question, but so far evidence has not provided a definite answer.

* Events outside Piedmont were moving rapidly. Revolutions in Sicily, Naples, Lombardy and Venetia broke out in rapid succession. In Austrian Lombardy the extreme revolutionaries wanted an independent republic while the moderates favoured union with Piedmont. Charles Albert saw advantages in putting himself at the head of a Lombard revolt against Austria, not least because there was a reasonable chance of eventually annexing Lombardy. He hesitated to take action, afraid that his absence in Lombardy would give revolutionaries a chance to stir up trouble in Genoa, the most vulnerable part of his kingdom. Public pressure and news that the revolutionary government of Venetia had voted for union with Piedmont persuaded the *Re Tentenua* (the wobbling King) to declare war on 23 March '. . . For the purpose of more fully showing by outward signs the sentiments of Italian unity, we wish that our troops should enter the territory of Lombardy and Venetia, bearing the arms of Savoy [the royal house of Piedmont] above the Italian tri-coloured flag'.

Historians have argued about whether Charles Albert did act only out of self interest. He certainly insisted that Lombardy and Venetia agree to be 'fused' with Piedmont as the price of his help. Or was he genuinely concerned to support a liberal revolt against the foreigner, Austria, and make himself leader of a nationalist movement? A year earlier he had written, 'Should providence call us to a war for the independence of Italy I will mount my horse and with my sons put myself at the head of my army . . . glorious will be the day on which we can raise the cry of a war of Italian independence'. But that was at a time when there was little chance of having to put his words into effect, and such a bold boast was easy to make.

The decision once made, Charles Albert entered the war with enthusiasm. Incompetently led by himself and ill prepared for war, his army of 60 000 crossed into Lombardy and occupied Milan. The city had already been evacuated by the Austrians, who waited for reinforcements and then defeated Charles Albert at Custoza on the border with Venetia. An armistice was signed and the Piedmontese army withdrew from Lombardy, leaving it again in Austrian hands.

Charles Albert broke the news to his people:

1  My army was almost alone in the struggle. The want of provisions forced us to abandon the positions we had conquered . . . for even the strength of the brave soldier has its limits. But the throbs of my heart were ever for Italian independence. People of the kingdom!

5   Show yourselves strong in a *first* misfortune . . . Repose confidence
in your king. The cause of Italian independence is not yet lost.

Early in 1849 having regrouped his forces and been persuaded, incor-
rectly, by the chief minister that Louis Napoleon, newly elected President of the French Republic, would come to his aid if Piedmont again
attacked Austria, Charles Albert re-entered the war. He was heavily
defeated by the Austrians at Novara in April. His declaration that Italy
would achieve independence and unity by her own efforts, 'Italia farà da
sè' (Italy will make herself by herself), was shown to be an empty boast.
While the military power of Austria remained supreme in the peninsula,
there was no way for Italy to gain independence or unity without outside
help.

*  One of the few survivors of the momentous years of 1848–9 was the
Piedmontese *Statuto* embodying the constitution. Charles Albert's
successor, Victor Emmanuel II has been traditionally seen as a
courageous figure defying Austrian plans for its abolition. Most historians now agree, however, that Victor Emmanuel himself was not
particularly anxious to perpetuate the constitution, but was pressured
into doing so by the Austrians, who were afraid that he would make
himself so unpopular by abolishing it, that the stability of the monarchy
in Piedmont would be threatened. In Austrian eyes, anything, even a
state with a moderately liberal constitution, was better than a republic.
So the constitution, such as it was, remained in force, and despite its
limitations gave an opportunity for active political life in Piedmont which
did not exist anywhere else in Italy. With a comparatively free press, an
elected if not very representative assembly, and a degree of civil liberty
and legal equality, Piedmont attracted refugees from other parts of Italy
during the next decade, which was dominated by the political leadership
of Cavour.

## 2 Cavour

Count Camillo Benso di Cavour was born in Piedmont in 1811 while it
was still under Napoleonic rule. He was the second son of a rich noble
family. His father, an intelligent and successful businessman, was a
minister in the absolutist government of Victor Emmanuel I. Cavour was
sent away to the Royal Military Academy when he was ten, where he
proved a rebellious student. Afterwards he was for a short time in the
service of the young Charles Albert, and then became an officer in the
army, where again he gained the reputation of being a troublesome rebel.
To get rid of him, he was sent to a frontier post, where boredom led him
to develop an interest in reading, mainly books on economics and
politics. He even began to imagine himself as Prime Minister of a united
Italy, a totally unrealistic dream in 1832, and not taken seriously by
anyone, especially as at the time he had no plans for going into politics.

*Victor Emmanuel's oath taking, 1849*

He left the army without regret in 1833, and the next year, not finding any employment to his taste, he set out to visit Paris and London. In Britain Cavour made a tour of the industrial areas, and was much impressed by the factories and mills be saw, and not at all put off by the smoke, dirt and squalor around him. He especially enjoyed the Liverpool–Manchester railway, the first passenger line in the world which had been opened only five years earlier. For the rest of his life railways remained an abiding interest.

In 1835 he returned to Piedmont, and for a while occupied himself with his other life long interest, gambling, on the stock exchange, in casinos and at cards. Then he took over the running of part of the family estate, taking an active and practical interest in the operation, importing artificial fertilisers from America and making use of new agricultural methods and machinery. For 13 years he lived on the estate, but continued his political and economic studies. He began writing articles on a wide range of subjects. In 1846 he wrote on his favourite subject, railways, which he described as the great marvel of the nineteenth century. As well as studying the railways in England, he investigated the way in which the London banks operated, and it was on his initiative that the Bank of Turin was set up in 1847, with himself as one of its first directors.

\* When Charles Albert freed the press from censorship in 1847, Cavour founded his own journal, *Il Risorgimento*, and used it to publish his ideas for the future of Piedmont and Italy. He welcomed the constitution granted by Charles Albert in 1848, for one of the first recommendations in *Il Risorgimento* had been for a moderate constitution. He stood for election to the first Piedmontese Parliament, but failed to win a seat, although he did so a few months later in a by-election. Once elected he soon made himself known as a liberal, non-revolutionary politician.

In October 1850 he was appointed minister of argriculture, commerce and the navy. He began by putting into operation his economic beliefs and made free trade treaties with France, Britain and Belgium. He even made one with Austria which allowed Piedmontese wines and other goods to be exported to Lombardy. D'Azeglio, the Prime Minister of the time, did not enjoy the details of administration and handed over much of the day to day government business to Cavour, who also became minister of finance in 1851, after he had been able to obtain better terms for a government loan to build a railway than the government itself had been able to do.

By 1852 Cavour found himself increasingly out of sympathy with the right wing government of d'Azeglio, and he made a political alliance with the leader of the moderate left wing party in Parliament, to form a new centre party. His decision was precipitated by a government proposal to reduce the freedom of the press slightly, which he feared might herald a return to absolutism.

By the end of May Cavour's position in d'Azeglio's government had become too difficult, and he resigned. He went abroad, finding time for a visit to Paris and a first meeting with Louis Napoleon, the President of the French Republic. While Cavour was away a crisis occurred involving the Church when the government decided to introduce civil marriage allowing couples to marry without a church service. There was strong opposition from the clergy. The Pope wrote to the King, and the king put pressure on Parliament to reject the bill. D'Azeglio resigned, and suggested Cavour as his successor, whereupon Victor Emmanuel asked Cavour to form a new government. He accepted, but was asked to agree to drop the civil marriage bill. Reluctantly he did so, and became Prime Minister in November 1852. He was to remain in office, apart from a few months in 1859–60, until his early death in 1861. These nine years were among the most momentous in the history of Italy.

* When Cavour became Prime Minister he had only a limited knowledge and understanding of foreign affairs. In the 1840s he had expressed a vague general wish that Italy should be united and free from Austrian domination, but too much should not be read into these remarks, for in the 1850s he referred on a number of occasions to the idea of Italian unity as 'rubbish'. Probably he did not come to accept it as a realistic possibility until after 1859.

He soon gained the experience in foreign affairs which he lacked in 1852, for almost immediately, in 1853, an international crisis erupted, which led to the outbreak of the Crimean war. Traditionally Cavour has been seen as happily entering the war against Russia in order to gain the friendship of Britain and France and to be sure of some of the spoils, as well as a seat at the eventual peace conference. The more recent and more convincing interpretation of his actions is that he was pressurized into the war by Britain and France, partly because more troops were needed and partly because Austria needed reassurance that if she joined the allied armies against Russia, Piedmont would not take advantage of the situation to stir up trouble in Lombardy.

Piedmont sent an army to the Crimea. It fought one battle with some success, and Cavour did attend the peace conference in Paris 1856. He gained nothing from it except a second meeting with Louis Napoleon, now the Emperor Napoleon III, but this was useful for they were to keep in touch during the next two years, not directly but through intermediaries, including Napoleon's nephew Prince Jerome-Napoleon, who became a close friend of Cavour.

## a) Plombières

These contacts bore fruit in July 1858 when Cavour was invited to meet Napoleon at Plombières, near the Swiss frontier. The meeting, which Napoleon seems to have initiated took place in great secrecy. Even the French Foreign Minister was not aware of what was happening. Hearing that Cavour had arrived in the town, the Foreign Minister sent a note to warn Napoleon. This reached him while he was actually talking with Cavour, who himself had been equally secretive. He had told only Victor Emmanuel and one other minister of the proposed meeting, which began to look like a conspiracy.

Whose were the proposals discussed at Plombières? Napoleon had issued the invitation and might therefore be assumed to have made the proposals, but there is some evidence that Cavour took a memorandum with him, which contained ideas very similar to what was eventually agreed.

Three days later, on 24 July, Cavour sat down and wrote a long and detailed letter to Victor Emmanuel giving his version of the discussion:

1 The ciphered letter which I sent Your Majesty from Plombières could give only a very incomplete idea of the long conversations I had with the Emperor. I believe you will be impatient to receive an exact and detailed narration. That is what I hasten to do having just
5 left France.

As soon as I entered the Emperor's study, he raised the question which was the purpose of my journey. He began by saying that he had decided to support Piedmont with all his power in a war against Austria, provided that the war was undertaken for a non-
10 revolutionary end which could be justified in the eyes of diplomatic circles – and still more in the eyes of French and European public opinion.

Since the search for a plausible excuse presented our main problem before we could agree, I felt obliged to treat that question
15 before any others. First I suggested that we could use the grievances occasioned by Austria's bad faith in not carrying out her commercial treaty. To this the Emperor answered that a petty commercial question could not be made the occasion for a great war designed to change the map of Europe. Then I proposed to revive
20 the objections we had made at the Congress of Paris against the illegitimate extension of Austrian power in Italy.

The Emperor did not like these pretexts. 'Besides,' he added, 'inasmuch as French troops are in Rome, I can hardly demand that Austria withdraw hers from Ancona and Bologna.' This was a
25 reasonable objection. . . .

My position now became embarrassing because I had no other precise proposal to make. The Emperor came to my aid, and together we set ourselves to discussing each state in Italy, seeking grounds for war. It was very hard to find any.
30 . . . We went on to the main question: what would be the objective of the war?

The Emperor readily agreed that it was necessary to drive the Austrians out of Italy once and for all. . . .

. . . But how was Italy to be organized after that? . . . The valley
35 of the Po, the Romagna, and the Legations would form a kingdom

of Upper Italy under the House of Savoy. Rome and its immediate surroundings would be left to the Pope. The rest of the Papal States, together with Tuscany, would form a kingdom of central Italy. The Neapolitan frontier would be left unchanged. These
40 four Italian states would form a confederation the presidency of which would be given to the Pope to console him for losing the best part of his States.

This arrangement seems to me fully acceptable. Your Majesty would be legal sovereign of the richest and most powerful half of
45 Italy, and hence would in practice dominate the whole peninsula. . . .

After we had settled the fate of Italy, the Emperor asked me what France would get, and whether Your Majesty would cede Savoy and the County of Nice. I answered that Your Majesty believed in
50 the principle of nationalities and realized accordingly that Savoy ought to be reunited with France; and that consequently you were ready to make this sacrifice, even though it would be extremely painful to renounce the country which had been the cradle of your family and whose people had given your ancestors so many proofs
55 of affection and devotion. The question of Nice was different, because the people of Nice, by origin, language, and customs, were closer to Piedmont than France. . . .

Then we proceeded to examine how the war could be won, and the Emperor observed that we would have to isolate Austria so that
60 she would be our sole opponent. That was why he deemed it so important that the grounds for war be such as would not alarm the other continental powers.

. . . Unless the Emperor is deluding himself, which I am not inclined to believe after all he told me, it would simply be a matter
65 of a war between France and ourselves on one side and Austria on the other.

The Emperor nevertheless believes that, even reduced to these proportions, there remain formidable difficulties. There is no denying that Austria is very strong. . . .
70 Success will thus require very considerable forces. The Emperor's estimate is at least 300,000 men, and I think he is right. . . . France would provide 200,000 men, Piedmont and the other Italian provinces 100,000. . . .

Once agreed on military matters, we equally agreed on the
75 financial question, and I must inform Your Majesty that this is what chiefly preoccupies the Emperor. Nevertheless he is ready to provide us with whatever munitions we need, and to help us negotiate a loan in Paris.

A provisional agreement was also reached for a marriage between Victor Emmanuel's daughter and one of Napoleon's cousins.

The arrangements reached at Plombières were largely incorporated in a secret treaty in January 1859, although there were some changes. Cavour's objections were overcome and Nice was added to Savoy as Napoleon's proposed reward, while the idea of an Italian confederation headed by the Pope was abandoned.

* To put the whole scheme into operation Cavour and Napoleon needed to provoke Austria into war. Cavour began by writing an emotional anti-Austrian speech for Victor Emmanuel to deliver at the opening of Parliament in January 1859, which included the words 'we cannot be insensitive to the cry of anguish (*grido di dolore*) that comes to us from many parts of Italy'. '*Grido di dolore*' quickly became a catchphrase throughout Italy to express popular anti-Austrian feelings.

Napoleon still insisted that in any war Austria must appear the aggressor, and this proved difficult to arrange. In despair, Napoleon even began to talk to Cavour of abandoning the idea of war, and substituting a congress of Great Powers to settle the Italian question. Cavour was not happy with this solution and wrote in reply to Napoleon III:

1   Your Majesty knows the difficulty of our position. We concerted a
    plan with your Majesty by which we would group around us all the
    live forces of Italy but without allowing our cause to be contami-
    nated by any revolutionary element. . . . If we are now
5   made to wait outside the door while others discuss the fate of Italy,
    in a Congress where Your Majesty plays the chief role, the rest of
    Italy will see us as feeble and powerless. Even in Piedmont opposi-
    tion will grow and it will be hard to go on governing without
    exceptional measures and the use of force.
10      I am not moved by any puerile vanity or exaggerated notion of
    our importance, it is just that our exclusion from a Congress would
    deprive us of our strength and prestige which we need for that great
    enterprise which is our duty and right and which would be the
    glory of your reign. . . . Austria has misjudged you and adopted a
15  menacing or even provocative tone. She is playing the role of an
    aggressor, and this makes me hope she will before long commit one
    of those aggressive acts which will justify your armed intervention.
    I hope so with all my heart.

Cavour's heartfelt wish was soon granted. In April 1859 Austria issued an ultimatum demanding unilateral demobilization by Piedmont. The Austrians had mobilized a large army in nothern Italy, but could not afford the expense of maintaining it for long. They dared not demobilize while Piedmont still had an army ready for war, and so took the dangerous step of sending the ultimatum. Cavour replied that Piedmont could not comply with the demand, and Victor Emmanuel immediately issued a proclamation: 'People of Italy! Austria assails Piedmont. . . . I fight for the right of the whole nation . . . I have no other ambition than to be the first soldier of Italian independence'. So the war began.

## b) The War of 1859

The start of the war was slow and marked by chaos and confusion. It took Napoleon several days to declare war in support of his ally, and then he needed time to transport his army to Italy by land and sea. When it did arrive, by train as befitted a modern army, it was badly organized, with insufficient tents, and even worse, with insufficient ammunition. The Austrian general was even slower in moving his troops than the allies, but eventually both sides were ready to start the fighting.

The war was short (only seven weeks), violent and horrible. Its result was decided in June by two battles, Magenta and Solferino. Both were major defeats for Austria. The casualty rate on both sides was very high, and conditions for the injured were appalling. There was no provision, not even any bandages for the wounded, who often lay, terribly maimed, on the battlefield for hours, without help and with death as their only hope.

* Suddenly on 11 July 1859, Napoleon made a truce with Austria. Although he seems to have been genuinely sickened by the carnage at Magenta and Solferino, there were other reasons for his actions. He feared that Prussia, whose troops had already been mobilized, might come to the aid of Austria if the war continued, and that the combined armies would be invincible. Even if this did not happen, the Austrian army alone was so strong it was unlikely that Napoleon would reach Venetia, let alone Vienna.

The most important reason, however, for Napoleon's decision to make peace was the result of events in Italy itself. On the first day of the war a working-class demonstration in Florence in Tuscany had led to the Grand Duke leaving for Vienna. A little later an upper-class group assumed control of the Duchy and announced that they wished Tuscany to be united with Piedmont. Revolution spread to Modena and Parma. In all these states Piedmontese officials and soldiers moved in and took over, setting up provisional governments. At the same time in the part of the Papal States known as the Romagna revolution was being encouraged by one of Cavour's agents. Napoleon distrusted Cavour's activities, especially in Tuscany, which had not been included in the Plombières scheme for Piedmontese expansion. As far as Napoleon was concerned Cavour was overstepping the bounds of the agreement. As a result, Napoleon met Franz Joseph, the young Austrian Emperor, to draw up terms for an armistice without consulting any representative of Piedmont.

The armistice is known as the armistice of Villafranca. By its terms Lombardy would be given to France to pass on to Piedmont, but Venetia would remain Austrian (see page 79). The idea of an Italian Confederation under the presidency of the Pope was resurrected. The rulers of Tuscany, Modena and Parma would be restored to their Duchies, though it was not made clear how this could be done, and in fact it was not carried out. Victor Emmanuel was persuaded to accept the terms, but Cavour was furious. Piedmont had been betrayed. After a hysterical interview with Victor Emmanuel he resigned.

\* During the next nine months, while Cavour was out of office, the fate of central Italy was decided. The provisional governments set up by Piedmont during the war began to arrange for the election of assemblies. In Tuscany the assembly, carefully rigged by the government, voted unanimously in August for annexation by Piedmont. A rather more democratically elected assembly in Modena also voted for union, as did the Romagna. Victor Emmanuel and his ministers, aware that Napoleon remained unsympathetic to this extension of Piedmontese territory, decided not to put the annexations into effect immediately. Provisional governments were left in control.

The armistice of August developed into a peace conference held in Zurich in November and this time Piedmont was invited to send representatives. The ceding of Lombardy first to France and then to Piedmont was confirmed. The problem of central Italy was shelved, to be dealt with by Napoleon's favourite means, a European congress, but this plan was sabotaged by a pamphlet published in Paris. It recommended the Pope not to press for an Italian Confederation, but to reconcile himself to the loss of most of the Papal States and settle just for the Patrimony, the area round Rome. When it was found that the pamphlet was an officially inspired government leak, written on the orders of Napoleon himself and representing his plans for the Papal States at the proposed congress, the Pope was shocked and angry. The Austrian government refused to take part in any congress which followed this line, and the idea of settling the question of the Central Italian states by Congress collapsed.

Partly as a result of this and partly as a result of pressure by Britain, Napoleon had become more sympathetic to the idea of the union of north and central Italy into a single state under the control of Piedmont by the time Cavour returned to power as Prime Minister early in 1860. One way of re-establishing good relations with Napoleon would be to implement the Plombières agreement to cede Savoy and Nice to France. Piedmont could have backed out of the part of the agreement, on the grounds that Napoleon had failed to free Venetia from the Austrians as promised. But if Napoleon were not given Savoy and Nice, Cavour knew he was very unlikely to agree to the formal annexation of Central Italy by Piedmont. The best way of saving everyone's face seemed to be a series of plebiscites in all the states concerned.

In mid March 1860, in Tuscany and in the new state of Emilia, made up of the Duchies of Modena and Parma together with the Romagna, plebiscites were held to see whether the population approved of union with Piedmont. The results were a foregone conclusion after the strenuous propaganda campaigns waged by the provisional governments. In Emilia, for instance, 427 512 voted for union with Piedmont, and 756 against. In Turin decrees were published declaring Tuscany and Emilia part of the kingdom of Piedmont.

A secret treaty between Victor Emmanuel and Napoleon in March ceded Savoy and Nice to France, subject to plebiscites in both places. These were held in April and again huge majorities voted in favour of annexation. The result in Savoy, which was French speaking, was not unexpected, but in Nice, which was Italian speaking, the results looked suspicious. There were 24 484 in favour and only 160 against. Cynics said that the presence of a French army in Nice at the time on its way home from Lombardy had something to do with the result. Garibaldi, who had been born in Nice and was one of its elected representatives in the Piedmontese parliament, certainly did not accept the accuracy of the figures. He was preparing a military expedition to prevent Nice being taken over by France, when he was diverted by an outbreak of revoltution in Southern Italy, in Sicily.

## 3 Cavour and Garibaldi

Historians have argued interminably about the motives of Cavour and Garibaldi in the events which followed, and about the relations between the two men. In every way they presented a contrast. Cavour, the nobleman, educated, intelligent, cool, calm and collected, the fat little politician and diplomat, and Garibaldi, rough, ill educated, impetuous, passionate, charismatic, the soldier – and leader of men, whose thought processes, simple and straightforward, were not allowed to get in the way of action. Garibaldi had come under the influence of Mazzini in 1831 and although he afterwards abandoned the republican ideals of Mazzini, he retained the nationalist ones, and became the leading champion of an independent and united Italy. All his actions were aimed at the expulsion of Austria and the formation of an Italian kingdom under the rule of Piedmont. These aims became an obsession and dominated his life.

How far Cavour was committed to the same aims is open to question. He certainly had written during the 1840s of the possibility of a united Italy, but the first suggestion that he was thinking seriously about it was in the letter which he wrote to Victor Emmanuel after the meeting at Plombières with Napoleon, and that is open to other interpretations. Cavour was realistic enough to know that there was no hope of Piedmont being able to expel Austria from nothern Italy without outside help, and the only available source of such help was France. He had reasoned that France would be prepared to help in the struggle up to a point and in return for certain rewards, such as Nice and Savoy. He also realized that France would not easily allow Piedmont to expand beyond the formation of a north Italian kingdom, and certainly not to lead a united Italy, for separate Italian states could be useful allies for France in any conflict with Austria, while a united Italy could pose a threat to France herself. For this reason France had been unwilling to encourage a take over by Piedmont of Tuscany and Emilia, and not until Napoleon changed his

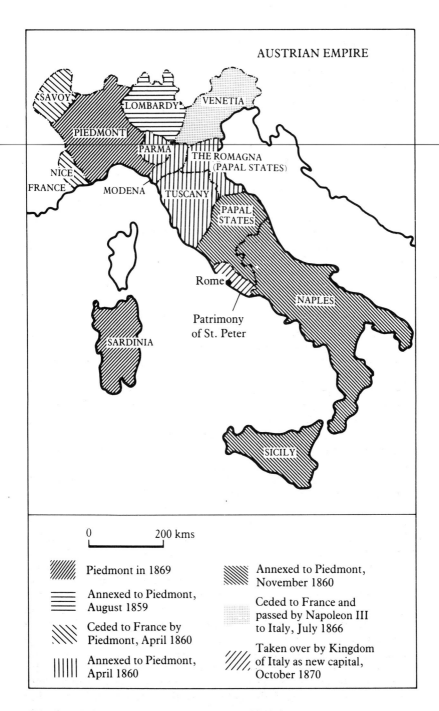

AUSTRIAN EMPIRE

SAVOY

LOMBARDY    VENETIA

PIEDMONT

PARMA

NICE          THE ROMAGNA
FRANCE        (PAPAL STATES)

MODENA    TUSCANY

PAPAL
STATES

Rome

Patrimony
of St. Peter          NAPLES

SARDINIA

SICILY

0          200 kms

////// Piedmont in 1869

===== Annexed to Piedmont,
      August 1859

\\\\\ Ceded to France by
      Piedmont, April 1860

||||| Annexed to Piedmont,
      April 1860

\\\\\ Annexed to Piedmont,
      November 1860

:::::: Ceded to France and
       passed by Napoleon III
       to Italy, July 1866

////// Taken over by Kingdom
       of Italy as new capital,
       October 1870

*The Unification of Italy, 1859–70*

mind about Piedmontese expansion in early 1860, did Cavour see the unification of Italy as a real possibility. Even then it is doubtful how far he was convinced that a totally united Italy was either possible or desirable. Piedmont had obtained control of northern Italy by diplomacy and limited war; anything more could only be gained by a major civil war. For Cavour enough was enough, and the time to stop had arrived.

Not so for Garibaldi. He wanted Rome and Venetia, Naples and Sicily, wanted them as part of a united Italy, and wanted them at once. His plan was for a military expedition to unite Italy through revolution in the south. (For details of Garibaldi's invasion of southern Italy, see Chapter III, page 64.)

Cavour's opinion of Garibaldi's plan is difficult to determine. Some historians believe that Cavour, either to conceal his true aims or to prevent foreign intervention, pretended to stop Garibaldi while secretly supporting him. This may have been because he thought of Garibaldi as an ally or because he intended from the start to use Garibaldi for his own purposes. Cavour was anyway in a difficult situation in Piedmont for elections were in progress and he feared that open opposition to Garibaldi would lead to a loss of popular support for the government. He needed to tread carefully. 'I omitted nothing to persuade Garibaldi to drop his mad scheme' wrote Cavour just before Garibaldi set out. When the success of the enterprise became clear in early August, Cavour admitted that he 'has rendered Italy the greatest services that a man could give her; he has given Italians confidence in themselves; he has proved to Europe that Italians know how to fight and die on the battlefield to reconquer a fatherland'. By this time even Cavour was talking of 'Italy' as though the peninsula had already been unified – a very great step forward politically for the cautious Cavour who, despite his earlier uncertainty, now saw that unification was probably inevitable whether he wished it or not.

Other historians see Cavour as Garibaldi's enemy, opposed to his plan to unify Italy, and therefore while pretending to help the expedition, secretly working to make sure it would fail. They believe that he disliked the whole idea of Garibaldi's expedition to attack Sicily and Naples. There was a very real chance that the expedition would fail, as similar ones had done before. If this happened Cavour, as Prime Minister would be blamed.

On a personal level, there is evidence that Cavour disliked Garibaldi, thought him stupid and did not entirely trust him. Garibaldi had been a republican and only later became a monarchist, giving his allegiance to Victor Emmanuel. Cavour remained uncertain whether this change of heart was genuine, thought Garibaldi was probably still a Mazzinian, and feared that if he were successful in southern Italy he might demand a republican Italy. At best this would lead to an Italy divided between a republican south and a monarchical north.

When Garibaldi's invasion of Sicily proved successful, Cavour decided to annex Sicily to Piedmont immediately. There were difficulties in doing this, for Sicily was part of the Kingdom of Naples and could not just be taken over by Piedmont, and while the Sicilians wanted independence from Naples they certainly did not want to replace Naples with Piedmont. While Cavour was considering what to do, news came that Garibaldi was marching north through Naples towards Rome.

Cavour may have believed, with some justification, that France and perhaps Austria would intervene if Garibaldi entered the Papal States. France had had a garrison in Rome since the fall of the Roman Republic, and any attack on the city would be sure to precipitate a conflict. He was also worried by the growing popularity of Garibaldi not only in Sicily and Naples, but in Piedmont itself, and feared that he might become the leader of a successful revolutionary coup and take over Piedmont. In that case, it was not impossible that Garibaldi could eventually take over the whole of Italy.

Cavour, therefore, organized an invasion of the Papal States by a Piedmontese army to intercept Garibaldi before he could reach Rome. It was more difficult than Cavour had expected to arouse popular support in the Papal States for the invasion and the Piedmontese army faced considerable opposition from the civilian population on its way south. When it finally met Garibaldi's army, all of southern and central Italy, except the area round Rome, came under the control of Piedmont, Cavour's decision to take the drastic step of invading the Papal States had been successful and had made the unification of Italy a reality (see map page 49).

Following his usual practice, Cavour arranged for plebiscites to be held, first in Naples and Sicily and afterwards in the Papal States. There were difficulties in Sicily, where most of the population was illiterate. These were overcome by providing two separate voting slips, one saying 'yes', the other 'no' and two separate ballot boxes also marked 'yes' or 'no'. The plebiscite asked *Italia una Vittorio Emmanuele?*', that is, 'should there be a united Italy under Victor Emmanuel?'. There was no mention of annexation by Piedmont, Victor Emmanuel was not identified as King of Piedmont, and the word '*Italia*' which had been Garibaldi's slogan during the fighting merely confused the question for most Sicilians who did not understand what was meant. Following careful preparations by Piedmont there was an overwhelming vote in favour.

In the eastern and central parts of the Papal States occupied by Piedmont, plebiscites were held in November 1860, and again enormous numbers voted in favour of annexation by Piedmont. In March 1861, the Kingdom of Italy was proclaimed, although it did not include quite all the peninsula; the Patrimony of St Peter, the area round Rome, remained under Papal control and in French occupation, while Venetia was still Austrian. Otherwise, unification was complete.

* How far was this due to Cavour? Although it has been established

that he does not seem to have considered Italian unification very seriously before the defeat of Austria in 1859, he was in contact with leaders of the National Society during the 1850s. This Society was a revolutionary group working for national unity, which by the mid 1850s was promoting the idea of an Italy united as a monarchy under Victor Emmanuel of Piedmont. There is no evidence, however, that before 1859 Cavour thought their proposals realistic. Then a succession of events – the defeat of Austria, the revolt in Sicily, Garibaldi's conquest of the south – changed the situation and led to Cavour's decision to invade the Papal States. Historians disagree about his motives for doing so. Was his intention simply to stop Garibaldi's threatened attack on Rome, because this, if successful, could have left Garibaldi as undisputed leader of Italy, and would in any case have led to difficulties with France, the protector of the Papacy? Or was he a political opportunist who saw the chance, by intervention in the Papal States, of bringing about a hoped for unification of Italy?

The evidence is not clear, but it does suggest that even in 1860 Cavour was not a committed nationalist. He seems to have felt that complete unification was neither necessary nor desirable. What he wanted was an Italy free from Austrian occupation, and the consolidation of Piedmontese power in the north. Union with the impoverished and backward south would only hinder Piedmont's development. The view of late nineteenth-century historians that Cavour was the patriot 'maker of Italy' has become less acceptable; more convincing is the view that he united Italy not so much as the result of intention or conviction but more through force of circumstances.

## 4 The Kingdom of Italy

On 27 January 1861 elections were held for the first Parliament of the new Kingdom of Italy. In March Victor Emmanuel was recognized as King of Italy. The new Parliament met in Turin, which remained the centre of power in Italy, for unification had been a take-over by Piedmont. Not only the constitution, but the Piedmontese legal and administrative systems were extended to, or more properly, imposed upon the rest of the country. The King retained his Piedmontese title of Victor Emmanuel II – he did not become Victor Emmanuel I of Italy.

No concessions were made to the susceptibilities of the other Italian states. They had been allowed to vote by plebiscite whether they wished to join Piedmont, but they were not allowed to discuss or vote on matters affecting the constitution. Cavour spoke of proposals for administrative changes, but no changes were actually made, and no effort was made to give more freedom or independence of action to the other states. There were no concessions to regional customs and traditions, or to economic or political differences. Centralized government, based on Piedmont, was finally established, and carried out throughout the kingdom by

Piedmontese civil servants, lawyers, politicians, and soldiers. All senior posts were filled by Piedmontese, who in many cases had little knowledge or understanding of the places or people they were administering.

Cavour was adamant that the limited constitutional monarchy of Piedmont must be imposed throughout a united Italy. He still feared the possibility of a radical republic, of the kind favoured by Mazzini, being set up in the south, and believed that such a division between north and south would eventually lead to civil war.

Ironically, it was Cavour's policy of rigid integration which itself led to civil war in the 1860s. In the south, in Sicily and Naples, the 'brigands' war broke out early in 1861. Disbanded troops of the former government united with dissatisfied peasants, and jointly attacked government offices and killed the Piedmontese officials they found there. The army retaliated, and a violent and brutal civil war followed, with great cruelty on both sides. Large numbers were killed, farm land was destroyed, trade came to a standstill and there was widespread unemployment.

Matters were made worse by local feuds and family vendettas. The south was politically and industrially backward, illiterate and poverty stricken. It was not ready for union with Piedmont. The demands made by such a union, with its constitution based on a restricted franchise and relying on the wealthy aristocratic or landowning families to operate it, was totally out of keeping with the needs of the impoverished South.

Cavour did not live to deal with the problems of the south or that of Rome, which most Italians thought of as the natural capital of Italy, but which was not yet part of the new Kingdom of Italy.

He died on 6 June, 1861 suddenly 'of a fever' which may have been malaria. Six weeks before, Garibaldi had made a dramatic speech in Parliament on behalf of the soldiers who had fought with him, in the course of which he had spoken violently against Cavour as an evil influence on Victor Emmanuel and as the man who had given away Savoy and Nice to France. Cavour had been deeply upset by this personal attack, for despite their differences he had come to respect Garibaldi's military skills, if not to agree with his political beliefs . He replied:

1   I know that between me and the honourable General Garibaldi there exists a fact [the cession of Savoy and Nice] which divides us like an abyss. . . . if he cannot forgive me this act I will not bear him any grudge for it.

Only a few months before his death he wrote in an often quoted letter:

1   I have never felt so weak as when Parliament is not in session . . . I am a child of liberty and owe it everything I am. If ever it should be necessary to forget the constitution, it will not be for me to do it. If ever Italians should need a dictator, they will choose Garibaldi, and
5   they will be right.

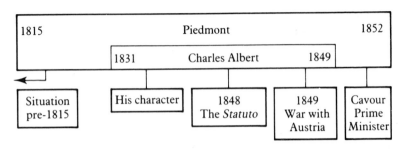

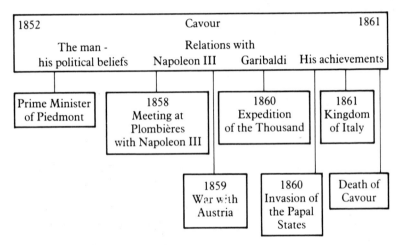

*Summary – Piedmont, Cavour and Italy*

---

**Making notes on** '*Piedmont, Cavour and Italy*'

Your notes on this chapter should help you understand the importance of Piedmont, and the part played by Cavour in the struggle for unification, both before and after he became Prime Minister in 1852.

The following headings and subheadings will help you:

1.    Piedmont
1.1.  Situation before 1815
1.2.  Genoa
1.3.  Charles Albert
1.4.  His policies
1.5.  Reforms

***

*Answering essay questions on 'Piedmont, Cavour and Italy'*

Much of the information in this chapter will be needed to answer general questions on the unification of Italy. These are discussed on pages 3–4 and 92–3.

You may find yourself having to answer a question specifically about Cavour, for he is the one individual associated with the *Risorgimento* about whom essay questions are regularly set.

The emphasis of such a question is likely to be on Cavour's intentions/ motives and whether they had changed by 1861. A typical example is:

'What were Cavour's ambitions for Italy in 1856 and how far had they changed by the time of his death?' (London, 1982)

Questions on Cavour often contain a quotation used as a 'challenging statement':

' "Cavour went further than he had intended towards the creation of a united Italy." Do you accept this view?' (Cambridge, 1981)

' "Cavour was a late and reluctant convert to the idea of Italian unification". Do you agree?' (Oxford and Cambridge, 1983)

Questions of this kind ask whether, in your opinion, the statement quoted is true. You need, therefore, to base your essay plan on the general pattern of either 'Yes, I agree. It is true because . . .', or 'No, I do not agree. It is not true, because . . .' But in each case you should also present any evidence that supports the opposite point of view.

Choose one of the 'challenging statement' questions above. Make a list of all the points you can think of that are relevant to the question. When your list is complete (and there could be as many as ten points on it) divide the points into two groups: those supporting the quotation and those that help to disprove it.

Think about the points in each group. Which argument seems the most convincing – for or against the statement?

Once you have decided this, you know which argument (agreeing with the quotation or disagreeing with the quotation) you are going to make the major part of the essay. But do not discard the minority argument. You could usefully employ it as your second paragraph.

So you should now have a plan that is along the lines of:

Paragraph 1 – Introduction (There are two sides to the argument etc.).

Paragraph 2 – Minority argument (It could be argued that . . . but on balance the contrary view is more convincing.)

Other paragraphs – One paragraph on each main point in the majority argument.

Final paragraph – Conclusion (Why the majority argument is generally most convincing.)

---

*Source-based questions on 'Piedmont, Cavour and Italy'*

### 1 Charles Albert's proclamation, August 1848

Read carefully the extract from Charles Albert's declaration of August 1848, given on pages 38–9. Answer the following questions:

a) The phrase 'Italian independence' appears twice in the extract. What does it suggest about the *extent* of Charles Albert's ambitions?

b) What two reasons does Charles Albert give for the withdrawal from Lombardy? What other reasons were significant in causing Piedmont's retreat?

c) What appear to be the purposes of Charles Albert's proclamation? Support your answer with evidence.

### 2 Victor Emmanuel's oath taking, 1849

Study carefully the print of Victor Emmanuel's oath taking, reproduced on page 40. Answer the following questions:

a) Describe and comment on three aspects of the events depicted in the print.

b) What emotions is the artist attempting to stir in the viewer? Support your answer with evidence.

c) What evidence does the print include to suggest that the artist actually witnessed the events he portrays? Explain your answer.

d) What are   i) the value and   ii) the limitations of prints of this type as historical evidence?

**3 Cavour's account of Plombières**

Read carefully the extract from Cavour's letter to Victor Emmanuel describing what happened at Plombières, given on pages 43–4. Answer the following questions:

a) Explain the significance of the phrase 'having just left France', (line 4).

b) Draw in diagramatic form (as a flow-diagram) the stages by which Cavour and Napoleon III hoped to engineer a war with Austria.

c) What was Napoleon III's reaction to Cavour's statement about the County of Nice? Is it likely that this reaction was genuine? Give reasons for your answer.

**Cavour's letter of March 1859**

Read carefully the extract from Cavour's letter of March 1859 to Napoleon III, given on page 45. Answer the following questions:

a) What course of action is Cavour arguing against in his letter?

b) What arguments does he use to support his case?

c) Which do you consider to be the least convincing of his arguments? Explain your answer.

d) What are the implications of the use of the word 'contaminated', (line 3)?

# CHAPTER 3

# Garibaldi and Italy

## 1 Garibaldi 1807–48

Today in this country, the name Garibaldi is hardly remembered at all. It may be known as the name of a currant biscuit, but for Victorian England the name was one to conjure with – the typical romantic hero, the swashbuckling adventurer, the national patriot, striking a blow for freedom. If this was the effect Garibaldi had on a country not his own, how much more was he likely to have dazzled his contemporaries in Italy!

His life was by any standards colourful and dramatic, and appears even more so in the highly imaginative memoirs and semi-autobiographical novels which he wrote towards the end of his life. He discribed his life as tempestuous, made up of good and evil, and that, at least, was true.

Guiseppe Garibaldi, the Italian patriot, was born a French citizen, in Nice in July 1807. He was, however, only eight when Nice again became part of Piedmont in the Vienna Settlement. In any case, his parents were Italian and he always regarded himself as Italian. His father was a sailor, and despite family pressure to enter the Church, Garibaldi joined the merchant navy. It was as a result of this that a chance encounter in 1831 in Marseilles brought him into contact with Mazzini, and altered the whole course of his life.

Mazzini, the founder of 'Young Italy', believed that Italy should not only be free and independent, but also united, not as a monarchy, but as a republic (see page 16). Probably his greatest gift was the ability to inspire revolutionary leaders with nationalist fervour and patriotic enthusiasm, and the greatest of his disciples was Garibaldi. Garibaldi was quickly converted to the dream of a united Italy, joined the 'Young Italy' movement and became involved in 1833 in Mazzini's revolutionary plot in Piedmont. The plot was intended to cause a mutiny in the army and navy, but it went wrong, and Garibaldi was among those sentenced to death.

Fortunately the sentence of execution could not be carried out, as Garibaldi had prudently left the country before the trial. Signing on as second mate he sailed for South America and settled in Rio de Janeiro. There he found that a branch of 'Young Italy' was already established. He joined it, and quickly became involved in revolutionary plans. But planning was not enough, he wanted action. He found it first as a pirate preying on the shipping of the New World, and then as a member of a rebel army in Brazil. In between campaigns he fell in love with the wife of a fisherman who became his devoted, but insanely jealous, companion for the next ten years.

After six years of fighting, Garibaldi retired to Montevideo in Uruguay to a humdrum existence as a commercial traveller selling spaghetti. He quickly became bored, and joined the army defending Uruguay against an Argentine take-over. He raised an Italian legion of guerrillas which fought with great bravery, if not with much military skill, and was largely responsible for the final Uruguayan victory. It was during this campaign that Garibaldi's men wore the uniform of the famous red shirt for the first time. Garibaldi was offered the rank of General at the end of the war. He refused it at the time, but later made good use of the title in Italy.

In 1848, hearing rumours of revolution in Italy, Garibaldi decided to return home, accompanied by sixty or so of his legionaries and some out of date weapons.

## 2 Garibaldi and the Revolutions of 1848–9

On his arrival in Nice, recruits flocked to join the Legion, and quickly came to be called 'The Garibaldini,' a name which was to become famous in the campaigns which followed. As their commander, Garibaldi was to establish himself as the greatest guerilla leader of the nineteenth century.

He presented a striking figure according to his contemporaries. A Dutch artist who saw him in Rome in April 1849 has left us this description:

1  Garibaldi entered through the gate. It was the first time I saw the man whose name everyone in Rome knew and in whom many had placed their hopes. Even now he is before my mind, as I saw him that first time. Of middle height, well made, broad shouldered, his
5  square chest, which gives a sense of power to his structure, well marked under the uniform – he stood there before us; his blue eyes, ranging to violet, surveyed in one glance the whole group. Those eyes had something remarkable, as well by their colour as by the frankness – I know no better word for it – of their expression.
10 They curiously contrasted with those dark, sparkling eyes of his Italian soldiers, no less than his light chestnut brown hair, which fell loosely over his neck onto his shoulders, contrasted with their shining black curls. His face was burnt red, and covered with freckles through the influence of the sun. A heavy moustache and a
15 light blonde beard ending in two points gave a martial expression to that open oval face. But most striking of all was the nose, with its exceedingly broad root, which has caused Garibaldi to be given the name of *Leone*, and, indeed, made one think of a lion; a resemblance which, according to his soldiers, was still more
20 conspicuous in a fight, when his eyes shot forth flames and his hair waved as a mane above his temples.

He was dressed in a red tunic with short flaps; on his head he wore a little black felt, sugar loaf hat, with two black ostrich feathers. In his left hand he had a light plain horseman's sabre, and
25 a cavalry cartridge bag hung down by his left shoulder.

*Garibaldi, 1849*

He often wore a white poncho, relic of his South American days and his portraits sometimes show him with a circle-brimmed hat tipped rakishly over one eye. His shapeless trousers he always made himself – he never mastered button holes and they had to be tied up with laces. His tastes were simple, and he ate sparingly. Rather rough in manner, generally good humoured and good company, he could also be ruthless and determined. His main interest, apart from fighting, was women of whom he collected a considerable number. Apart from the three he married, he had innumerable mistresses.

Scandal and gossip followed him everywhere, but could not obscure his ability as a guerilla leader nor his devotion to the cause of Italian unity. He in turn inspired devotion bordering on the fanatical among his men, and a near-religious adoration among the ordinary people. Street songs, ballads and popular prints of the time show Garibaldi as semi-divine, the equivalent of a local patron saint. His picture was often put alongside that of the Madonna. His charisma was overwhelming.

* When he first arrived in Nice, Garibaldi immediately offered his services to Charles Albert, King of Piedmont. The King mistrusted the offer, refused to see Garibaldi and sent him to the War Minister. Nobody wanted the Garibaldini, until the Revolutionary Committee of Milan in Lombardy asked for their help. With extra recruits a legion of 5000 men was established, but before it could go into action news of the defeat of Piedmont at Custoza arrived and most of the legionaries deserted. Those who remained fought a number of skirmishes in the last days of the campaign. When it was over the Garibaldini, despite several minor military successes against the Austrians, found that no government would accept their services. Later an Austrian general remarked that the one man who could have helped the Italians win the 1848 war, was the one man they turned their backs on.

The fact that Garibaldi had offered his services to Charles Albert was remarkable. It marked another turning point in his life. Garibaldi believed that only Charles Albert, could defeat the Austrians and unite Italy. So he abandoned all the republican principles he had learnt from Mazzini (although he kept his opposition to the Catholic Church) and became a royalist, all in the cause of Italian unity.

His change of heart appears to have been quite sincere. 'I was a Republican, but when I discovered that Charles Albert had made himself champion of Italy, I swore to obey him and faithfully to follow his banner'. Mazzini was deeply hurt by Garibaldi's change of allegiance and felt that Garibaldi had betrayed the revolutionary cause by going over to Charles Albert. Even Charles Albert himself was not over enthusiastic about his new follower. Only single-minded devotion to the cause of Italian unity can explain Garibaldi's action. He was, after all, an essentially practical man, more given to action than to thought, and was certainly a realist. He had the simple determination to achieve his aims by the best means available. Mazzini remained an idealist and he and

Garibaldi parted company politically, although they were to work together in the heroic defence of the Roman Republic.

## a) The Roman Republic

The Roman Republic was proclaimed in February 1849 after the Pope refused to grant further political concessions, and was forced to escape from Rome to safety in southern Italy (see page 25). The Republic was short lived, only surviving for four months in all. Administration was in the hands of the Triumvirate, three men led by Mazzini. Under his influence, the Republic was conducted according to the highest ideals of the liberal movements.

Garibaldi and the legionaries arrived in Rome as the city prepared, in the words of Mazzini, 'to resist, resist whatever the cost, in the name of independence, in the name of honour and the right of all states, great or small, strong or weak, to govern themselves'. The Pope had appealed for help from Austria and Spain, but the decisive attack on the Republic when it came was not from these Catholic monarchies but was ordered by the President of another republic, Louis Napoleon of France.

A French expeditionary force arrived at the gates of Rome, but was driven back. During a temporary truce French reinforcements were brought up, while Garibaldi made use of the lull to drive off a Neapolitan attack. But in the end, with the defenders heavily outnumbered by the besieging forces, the fall of Rome was a foregone conclusion. Garibaldi's legionaries fought heroically, but without much tactical skill and on 3 July the Republic fell.

Before that, on 30 June, Garibaldi had made a theatrical entrance into the Assembly meeting, with a sword so bent and battered from hand to hand combat it would no longer fit in the scabbard. He announced that further resistance was impossible. The Assembly appointed him Dictator of Rome to make what arrangements he thought necessary. He outlined his possible courses of action to the Assembly: to surrender the city (impossible), to continue the fight inside the city (suicidal in view of the greatly reinforced French army now numbering about 20 000, twice the size of the defending army), or to withdraw with as many men as possible towards Venetia, where the Republic there was still holding out against an Austrian army (the only acceptable option).

Garibaldi appealed to the crowd in the Piazza of St. Peter:

1　Fortune who betrays us today will smile on us tomorrow. I am going out from Rome. Let those who wish to continue the war against the stranger, come with me. I offer neither pay, nor quarters, nor provisions; I offer hunger, thirst, forced marches,
5　battles and death. Let him who loves his country in his heart and not with his lips only, follow me.

He collected nearly 5000 men, almost all his soldiers who had not been killed in the defence of Rome, and began a forced march towards the Adriatic coast. This march became one of the epic tales of the *Risorgimento*. Over 800 kilometres of mountainous country, a shortage of food and water, pursuit by enemy troops all took their toll, and only 1500 men reached the coast. Garibaldi's common law wife, who had accompanied him everywhere during the past ten years and often fought alongside him, died on the way and he was unable to stop long enough to bury her. Many of the Garibaldini were killed or captured, or deserted to become bandits. Garibaldi himself escaped to Genoa where he was arrested, but later freed on condition he left Italy at once. His career as a revolutionary soldier-hero seemed to be over, the drama played out, the legend finished, as he once again set sail across the Atlantic, but this time to North America.

## 3 Garibaldi 1849–59

In the United States he found what employment he could, eventually returning to sea as master of a ship on the China run, until he inherited some money from his brother. He used this to buy half of the small island of Caprera off the coast of Sardinia. There he took up farming but was able to keep in touch with affairs in Italy, through the National Society, which was working for the unification of Italy as a monarchy, under the leadership of Piedmont and its King (see page 52).

In the ten years since Garibaldi had left Italy there had been many changes. The situation in Piedmont was greatly altered. Charles Albert had been succeeded by his son, Victor Emmanuel, who was very different from his father. He was a pleasant, easy going man, lazy and often rather coarse in manner. He could be charming if he chose, liked a joke and enjoyed life as it came. He was not unlike Garibaldi in his down to earth, honest approach, but was much more politically able than he appeared. He managed, sometimes by sharp practice, to keep on good terms both with Garibaldi and with Cavour. He was to inspire great loyalty from Garibaldi, but there is some doubt about Victor Emmanuel's feelings for Garibaldi in return.

The leading exponent of the Italian cause was now Victor Emmanuel's chief minister, Cavour. Cavour's views on Italian unity were very far from those of the republican Mazzini and the other revolutionaries of the 1830s and 1840s. Indeed before 1860, he did not believe that a politically unified Italy was a realistic possibility (see page 48).

* After the discussions with Napoleon III at Plombières (see page 42). Cavour sent an invitation to Garibaldi through the National Society to visit Turin. There he met Cavour and Victor Emmanuel, and was given details of the plans for war against Austria in the spring of 1859. Garibaldi at once offered to enrol and train volunteers. He had now totally abandoned Mazzini, and threw in his lot with Victor Emmanuel whole heartedly.

\* In the spring of 1859, the Second War of Independence against Austria began. The armies of France and Piedmont were badly organized, the Austrian army even more so, and French and Piedmontese troops were able to conquer Lombardy. Garibaldi's men played an important part in the fighting in northern Italy, and he himself was presented by Victor Emmanuel with the Gold Medal for Valour, the highest military decoration in Piedmont.

Early the following year, Lombardy and the central Italian states, taken over by Piedmont during the war, were officially annexed and became part of the new North Italian kingdom, ruled over by Victor Emmanuel (see page 48). As part of the bargain with Napoleon III, Piedmont had to give up Savoy and Nice to France. The cession of Nice, the city of his birth, was a severe blow to Garibaldi, which embittered his relations with Cavour until the latter's death. Victor Emmanuel was now king of all of the northern half of Italy except Venetia. To Garibaldi it seemed as if the moment for the final liberation of Italy had arrived, and he began collecting money for a million rifles to be available when needed. The moment was indeed not far off, and the unification of Italy was about to become a reality.

## 4 Garibaldi and the Thousand

In April 1860 a revolt started in Palermo in Sicily against the King of Naples. It was almost certainly organized by followers of Mazzini and supported by the National Society, which had contacts throughout Italy. At the time Garibaldi was organizing an armed expedition to save Nice from being ceded to France. This was to be done by blowing up the ballot boxes to be used in the plebiscite. He was diverted from this plan by news of the revolt in Sicily. He began to collect more volunteers together and by early May 1860 had a force of about 1200, mostly very young men, who were known as 'The Thousand'. He also had with him his mistress and a thousand rifles, but no ammunition, aboard two old paddle steamers in the port of Genoa, ready to sail in the name of 'Italy and Victor Emmanuel' in support of a revolt which it was already known had failed. Other revolts elsewhere in Sicily were however still in progress.

Commonsense suggested that the expedition was not likely to be successful. It had been put together too quickly, the number of men was too small, their resources poor, the enemy forces were known to be large and previous expeditions of this kind had failed, including a much larger one in 1857. Garibaldi was a brilliant leader of men but no military tactician and was often unpredictable. On top of this, Cavour was not convinced that it was desirable to attempt to conquer Sicily, even if the task was within Garibaldi's abilty. The south was poor and backward and in Cavour's opinion not ready for amalgamation with Piedmont. In any case, he feared that foreign governments might be tempted to interfere if too much was done too quickly. He refused Garibaldi's request for arms and equipment for the expedition, and made it clear that it went without Piedmontese official support.

Later reports even suggested that Cavour tried to persuade Victor Emmanuel to arrest Garibaldi, but was too late, for the expedition had already sailed. A note from Cavour to his confidential agent in Paris makes it clear that he made 'every effort to persuade Garibaldi to drop his mad scheme', but could not take open action to stop him because of popular opinion and pressure from Victor Emmanuel. In the end Cavour could comfort himself with the idea that if the expedition failed, he would be rid of Garibaldi, 'a troublesome fellow', and if it succeeded 'Italy would get some benefit from it.'

Within a week Garibaldi had landed unopposed at Marsala in Sicily. From there he and his men advanced on Palermo, gathering recruits on the way and defeating a Neapolitan army in a hand-to-hand battle. In pouring rain 'The Thousand', now near 3000, reached Palermo, and found 20 000 enemy troops waiting for them. By outflanking these troops and with help from the townspeople, Garibaldi quickly took Palermo. The garrison withdrew to Naples, and Sicily was his. His task had been made easier by the fact that as a result of the earlier revolt by Sicilian peasants, the centre of the island was in a state of chaos, with bands of peasants seeking revenge against Neapolitan troops, and attacking the oppressive landlords. The speedy defeat of the Neapolitan army was due partly to Garibaldi's dashing and bold style of leadership, and partly to the poor leadership shown by the Neapolitan officers and to their soldiers' fear of ambush by the Sicilian bandits.

\* Garibaldi appointed himself 'Dictator' of Sicily and at first was sympathetic to the aims of the peasant revolt. He abolished the tax collected on corn being milled into flour which was a standing grievance of the peasants, and won their support by promising a redistribution of land. Soon, though, he changed sides and suppressed a number of new peasant revolts. As a result he won the support of the landowners, though he lost that of the peasants. This was essential as his main need was to restore law and order and for that he needed the help of the landowners. Without reasonable peace and stability in the island, Garibaldi could not proceed to his next step, which was to use Sicily as a jumping-off ground for an attack on the mainland and the next stage of the unification of Italy. His obsession with a united Italy had caused him to abandon the Mazzinian principles of supporting the underprivileged.

As part of his law and order campaign, Garibaldi introduced Piedmontese laws into Sicily as a preparation for annexation by Piedmont, but for the momemt he refused to hand over Sicily to Victor Emmanuel. He was afraid that if he did so, Cavour would stop him using Sicily as a base for the campaign against Naples. Cavour was undoubtedly surprised at Garibaldi's success in Sicily and probably displeased at the public acclaim. Garibaldi was too much in the limelight and likely to take too much of the credit himself for uniting Italy if he continued unchecked.

Cavour would have preferred things done more quietly, more constitutionally and the credit to go to Piedmont and Victor Emmanuel. He wrote to the Piedmontese ambassador in London:

1   In Sicily, Garibaldi has let himself become intoxicated with his success. Instead of carrying out annexation [to Piedmont] or allowing it to be carried out, he dreams of conquering Naples and delivering Italy.

There is more than a hint of jealousy here.

 * Cavour tried to arrange a revolution in Naples in favour of Victor Emmanuel before Garibaldi could get there, but it was unsuccessful. Orders were given to the Piedmontese navy to stop Garibaldi and his men from crossing the Straits of Messina to the mainland. Victor Emmanuel sent his orderly officer to Sicily with a letter to Garibaldi ordering him not to cross to the mainland. Years later a second letter, an unopened one, was found among the orderly officer's papers. This second letter was also from Victor Emmanuel, and told Garibaldi to take no notice of the first one. Why it was not opened is not known; it may not even have been delivered. But it seems that Victor Emmanuel was trying to be on the side of both Cavour and Garibaldi at the same time.

Typically, Garibaldi solved the problem by speed. Dodging the ships sent to intercept him, he ferried his men across the Straits to Calabria. Although heavily outnumbered, he fought his way north towards Naples. When he heard that the King of Naples had left the city, he accepted its surrender, arriving there, ahead of his troops, by train and almost alone.

For the next two months Garibaldi ruled as Dictator over the Kingdom of Naples, unable to advance any further because of a Neapolitan military stronghold in the north. Garibaldi's plan to march on through the Papal States to Rome and so complete the geographical unification of Italy was held up long enough for Cavour to act.

 * These dramatic successes of Garibaldi in southern Italy were not much to Cavour's liking. He believed that an attack on Rome, such as that planned by Garibaldi, would mean trouble, particularly with France. Napoleon III had been upset a couple of months earlier, when, on his way to Sicily, Garibaldi had landed a small diversionary force in the Papal States. The expedition had fizzled out, but the warning was clear. France and the rest of Catholic Europe could be expected to take action if Rome or the Pope's safety were threatened.

In addition, Cavour was aware that many of the men who had now joined Garibaldi (the numbers had swelled from 'The Thousand' to nearly sixty times that number) were Mazzinians. This meant that they were opposed to the Church and its teachings and would be very willing to join in an attack on Rome. Also, the Mazzinians were republicans and there was a danger that the whole nationalist movement would slip away from the leadership of Piedmont and its king and become again revolutionary and republican. However committed Garibaldi might have been to the cause of 'Italy and Victor Emmanuel', there must have been a doubt about how far even he could maintain control over his army of irregulars.

Cavour had to stop Garibaldi attacking Rome, the only way was to send an army from Piedmont through the Papal States to meet him before he could reach the city. Using the excuse that the Pope was unable to deal with a threatened revolt in his territory, the Piedmontese army, with Victor Emmanuel at its head marched through the Papal States. They defeated a Papal army on the way, and any civilians resisting the invasion were shot as traitors to the cause of a united Italy.

In October the Piedmontese reached Neapolitan territory and Victor Emmanuel and Garibaldi met in what should have been a dramatic scene, but proved to be something of an anti climax.

With a flourish of his broad-brimmed hat, Garibaldi saluted Victor Emmanuel as 'the first King of Italy'. The reply was an anticlimax: 'How are you, dear Garibaldi?'

Plebiscites were held in Sicily, Naples, Umbria and the Papal Marches and not surprisingly showed an overwhelming wish for annexation by Piedmont – there seemed to be no acceptable alternative, and nationalist enthusiasts were in the majority anyway after all the excitements of the summer.

* On 7 November, Victor Emmanuel and Garibaldi rode together in a triumphal state entry into Naples. One of the staff from the French Embassy in Piedmont wrote an account of the event:

1    The immense popularity Victor Emmanuel enjoys in the old provinces of Piedmont owes more to the monarchical sentiments of the people than to the personal qualities of the King. Events and above all the genius of his Prime Minister have raised him to the
5    position he now occupies in Italy and Europe. If ever his name becomes famous in history, his only glory will have been 'to have allowed Italy to create herself'.

Like all mediocre men, Victor Emmanuel is jealous and quick to take offence. He will find it difficult to forget the manner of his
10    triumphal entry into Naples, when, seated in Garibaldi's carrige — Garibaldi in a red shirt – he was presented to his people by the most powerful of all his subjects. People are mistaken in crediting Victor Emmanuel with a liking for Garibaldi. As soldiers they probably have points of contact in their characters and tastes, which have
15    allowed them to understand each other at times, but the hero's familiarity is very displeasing to the King. After all what sovereign, placed in the same situation, would not resent the fabulous prestige of Garibaldi's name?

The day after the state entry into Naples, Garibaldi handed over officially all his conquests to Victor Emmanuel, who in return offered him the rank of Major General, the title of Prince, a large pension and even a castle. Garibaldi refused them all, because of what he considered unfair treatment of his Red Shirts. The King had refused to inspect the troops and had not signed the proclamation of thanks sent to them. Soon afterwards the Garibaldini were disbanded. As Garibaldi said, 'They think men are like oranges; you squeeze out the last drop of juice and then you throw away the peel.'

Garibaldi retired to Caprera with a year's supply of macaroni and little else. Both Victor Emmanuel and Cavour were determined that Garibaldi should leave active political life; as far as they were concerned, his job was done. All Italy, except Rome and Venetia had been united under Victor Emmanuel and the constitution of Piedmont had been extended to the whole of the new Kingdom of Italy.

## 5 Garibaldi and Rome

Rome was still occupied by French troops, and there was continuing pressure from Italian liberals for it to be freed and incorporated into the new Italian Kingdom as the historical capital. Garibaldi had always maintained that whenever the government for political reasons found itself unable to promote national unity, it was the right of volunteers to take independent action.

What happened next is not clear, for the evidence is conflicting as so often in the story of Garibaldi, but in 1862 he returned to Sicily from Caprera and collected together about 3000 volunteers for the conquest of Rome. Apparently with the approval of Victor Emmanuel, but not that of the government, Garibaldi set off on the march north. He did not know that the Prime Minister, Cavour's successor, had planned a similar coup to that of 1860. The plan needed French agreement to an invasion of Papal territory by a Piedmontese army which would reach Rome before Garibaldi. But the plan failed because the French could not be persuaded to agree to it.

Meanwhile Garibaldi had been joyously received in Palermo with cries of 'Rome or Death'. Victor Emmanuel immediately issued a proclamation, withdrawing his support and disowning the whole operation. No one tried to stop Garibaldi, for the government had failed to tell the army to do so, and the message to the new naval commander at Messina was so vague that he allowed Garibaldi's troops to cross to Calabria. There, in bad weather, they were shot at by local troops and forced into the mountains. Most of the men deserted, and only 500 remained. They were defeated at Aspromonte in a short battle with government troops. Garibaldi was wounded in the leg, and captured. He was imprisoned for a time, and was then returned to Caprera.

The whole adventure was a disaster for Garibaldi personally and militarily – he was not used to being wounded nor defeated – and it was an acute embarrassment to the government, that the old hero, one of those responsible for the unification of Italy, had been defeated and imprisoned by the government of the kingdom he had helped to create.

* All was not quite over as far as Garibaldi was concerned. In 1864 the Italian government agreed to protect Rome from attack and to move the Italian capital from Turin in Piedmont to Florence in Tuscany, an indication that they had given up the idea of making Rome the capital of the kingdom. In return, the French withdrew from Rome. Garibaldi regarded this agreement as a betrayal of the Italian cause and raised yet another army, in 1867, to capture Rome and 'abolish the Pope'.

Garibaldi and his men marched towards Rome, but he was arrested and imprisoned on government orders, despite the fact that he had apparently been given government backing for the expedition. The Garibaldini continued, leaderless, towards Rome and suffered a series of defeats by the Papal army. Garibaldi, after several attempts, escaped in a dinghy from Caprera where he was under house arrest and disguised as a fisherman reached the mainland, and retook command of his men. Unfortunately the planned revolution among the Roman people failed to materialize on the date arranged, but Garibaldi was encouraged by his defeat of a Papal army. Immediately Victor Emmanuel disowned the expedition and the French government sent back to Rome an army equipped with the new breech loading rifles. They were decisive and the Garibaldini were totally defeated. It was the end of Garibaldi's part in Italian history, but not the end of his active life.

In 1870, after the defeat of Napoleon III by the German army and the fall of the Second French Empire, Garibaldi offered his services to the new French Republic. The French government was hesitant. After all Garibaldi was 63 years old, crippled with arthritis and still suffering from the wound received at Aspromonte. He did not seem the ideal choice for a military leader, but under pressure from public opinion the French government appointed him General of the Vosges army – a hotchpotch of sharpshooters and other irregular troops, who nevertheless under Garibaldi's leadership defeated the Germans in three small battles.

He was elected to the French National Assembly in recognition of his services, but finding considerable antagonism from his fellow members, he returned to his home on the island of Caprera where he remained until his death in 1882.

Meanwhile Rome had been attacked and captured in 1870 by Italian troops. Garibaldi was distressed that the government had taken advantage of the misfortunes of Napoleon III. He felt it was unsporting. As always his political sense was limited.

## 6 Garibaldi's Achievements

Garibaldi's contribution to the cause of Italian unity was very considerable. His flamboyant character, his striking appearance, his legendary adventures both inside and outside Italy made him a focal point for patriotic sentiment and emotion. He represented a non-intellectual, active approach to Italian unity, very different from that of Cavour.

As a military leader he was a good, sometimes brilliant commander, excellent at sizing up the situation, decisive and determined. A guerilla fighter *par excellence*, he and his men were best at hand-to-hand fighting, surprise night attacks and ambushes by day. He relied on his personality rather than strict discipline to maintain control over his men. Regular Italian officers who visited his camp on the outskirts of Rome in 1849 were shocked by the informality of the Garibaldini. One of them wrote:

1   Garibaldi and his officers were dressed in scarlet blouses, with hats of every possible form, without distinctions of any kind, or any pretension to military ornament. They rode on [South] American saddles, and seemed to pride themselves on contempt for all the
5   observances most strictly enjoined on regular troops . . . they might be seen hurrying to and fro, now dispersing, then again collecting, active, rapid and indefatigable. . . . We used to be surprised to see officers, the General himself included, leap down from their horses and attend to the wants of their own steeds. . . . If
10   they failed in procuring provisions from neighbouring villages, three or four colonels and majors threw themselves on the backs of their horses and armed with long lassoes, set off in search of sheep or oxen. . . .
    Garibaldi, in the meanwhile, if the encampment was far from the
15   scene of danger, lay stretched out under his tent [made from his unrolled saddle]. If the enemy were at hand, he remained constantly on horseback, giving orders and visiting outposts; often, disguised as a peasant, he risked his own safety in daring reconnaissances. . . . When the General's trumpet gave the signal
20   to prepare for departure, the lassoes served to catch the horses which had been left to graze at liberty in the meadows. . . . Garibaldi appeared more like the chief of a tribe of Indians than a General, but at the approach of danger, and in the heat of combat, his presence of mind and courage were admirable.

Garibaldi inspired great enthusiasm and devotion in his men, firing them with the same passionate beliefs in Italian unity that he had himself – at least while fighting was available. During periods of inaction, if things became bad, they showed a regrettable tendency to desert. Garibaldi's relaxed style of leadership and the lack of discipline among the Garibaldini probably made this inevitable.

Mobility is important in guerilla warfare, and unlike regular troops the Garibaldini wore a lightweight uniform of a shirt (the famous Red Shirt), loose trousers, boots, a cape and a broad-brimmed hat. They carried a black haversack and were armed with muskets or old rifles, sometimes with lances. In their belts they all wore a heavy poniard or dagger. They needed to travel light for Garibaldi's strategy included a good deal of marching backwards and forwards to confuse the enemy and a lot of running about with bayonets.

A contributory factor to Garibaldi's military success was the incompetence and lack of enthusiasm shown by the enemy. In Naples the King and his troops were so frightened by what Garibaldi had already achieved in Sicily that they put up little resistance. In Sicily itself he had been helped in his campaign by the general confusion on the island following the peasants' revolt, and by local hatred of the remaining Neapolitan troops who had gained an unenviable reputation for cruelty.

Nevertheless his conquest of the south was a remarkable achievement and a major element in the unification of Italy. He and his men accomplished it almost unaided and in a very short space of time against all odds and all expectations.

Whether it was desirable or wise to unite north and south in this sudden and violent way is another matter. There was support in the south for liberation from the rule of an oppressive and absolute monarchy but not necessarily a wish for unity with the north. Most of Garibaldi's men, like himself, came from the north and had little understanding of or sympathy for the impoverished and backward south. If Garibaldi had not been so anxious to move north as quickly as possible, more might have been done for the peasants instead of, as in Sicily, abandoning them to the landlords. An opportunity was missed to win popular support through agrarian reform. If the conquest of Naples too had been less speedy, and if the relations between Cavour and Garibaldi had been better, some alternative to the immediate introduction of the unsuitable Piedmontese administrative and legal systems into southern Italy might have been found.

All Garibaldi's actions can be explained by his total devotion to the idea of Italian unity. It became the driving obsession of his life and as a result he sometimes appeared unprincipled. From a republican follower of Mazzini he became a royalist follower of Charles Albert and later of Victor Emmanuel; from a supporter of popular revolution he became a supporter of the established regime. In each case he acted in what he considered the best interests of Italian unity. He could have established himself without difficulty as dictator of an independent southern Italy, but he believed national unity to be more important.

That chance meeting with Mazzini in 1833 had changed his whole life, giving him a cause to fight for. The ideals of 'Young Italy' appealed to the romantic side of his nature:

1   . . . without unity there is no true nation, without unity there is no real strength and Italy surrounded as she is by powerful, united and jealous nations, has need of strength above all things . . .

Resounding phrases like these fired his imagination and gave him a purpose. Without it he would have been merely a good leader of men, and one who, energetic and personally courageous, just enjoyed fighting.

As it was he was much more than that.

Even so he had his limitations. He was not very well educated and was not much of a thinker. His greatest weakness was probably his impetuosity. He acted first and thought afterwards, if at all, for his actions were dominated by his heart not his head. His understanding of politics was limited, as was his interest in them. As a result he was seldom aware of the effect which his actions might have on international relations, as in his plans to march on Rome in 1860, 1862 and 1867. Even if he had been so aware, it is doubtful whether he would have been concerned. He would have considered international repercussions a small price to pay for national unity.

---

### Making notes on 'Garibaldi and Italy'

Your notes on this chapter should give you a clear understanding of the part played by Garibaldi in the unification of Italy and the reasons for his actions.

The following headings should help you:

1.   Garibaldi 1807–48
2.   Garibaldi and the Revolutions of 1848–9
2.1. Garibaldi the man
2.2. 1848
2.3. The Roman Republic
3.   Garibaldi 1849–59
3.1. 1849–58
3.2. 1859
4.   Garibaldi and the Thousand
4.1. Invasion of Sicily
4.2. Control of Sicily
4.3. Conquest of Naples
4.4. Papal States
4.5. Garibaldi and Victor Emmanuel
5.   Garibaldi and Rome
5.1. 1862
5.2. 1867
6.   Garibaldi's Achievements

---

### Answering essay questions on 'Garibaldi and Italy'

Much of the material in this chapter will be needed to answer general questions on the unification of Italy, which are discussed on pages 3–4. It

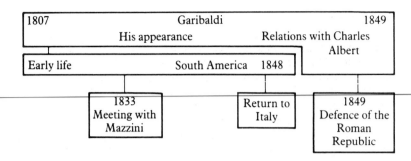

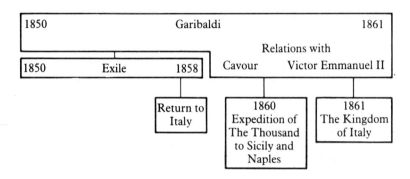

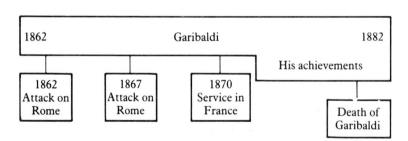

*Summary – Garibaldi and Italy*

will also be useful in providing additional evidence needed to answer
questions on Cavour, discussed on pages 55–6.

You will seldom find yourself writing an essay solely on Garibaldi.
Even those questions which appear to be concerned only with him
involve other issues. A typical example is:

'How important to the cause of Italian unification was the contribution of Garibaldi?' (JMB, 1981)

In dealing with a question which starts 'How important was the contribution of . . .' you will need to plan a two-part essay. The general pattern for such an essay is usually along the lines of either 'Yes, it was important because . . . but other contributions were also important because . . .' or 'No it was not very important because . . . other contributions were more important because . . .'

Having decided which approach is the right one, draw up your list of points for the contribution named in the question, and then your list for 'other contributions', and arrange them in order of importance.

You might now like to draw up an outline plan for this question.

First of all, list the contributors to Italian Unification. Would you include only named people in this list or would you also wish to include groups or situations? Why?

Secondly, for each contributor in turn, list the main ways in which he, they, or it contributed (Napoleon III might be easier for you to think through when you have read the next chapter). For example, your list on Cavour might include statements such as 'he gained French support for war against Austria', and 'he ensured that the Great Powers did not intervene to prevent central and southern Italy being united with Piedmont'.

Now you are ready to decide which of the two general approaches described above best fits the points you have to make. Decide this and write down the order in which you will present your points.

When you have done this, compare your plan with those of other members of your group. Look especially at the proportion of each essay that is planned to be devoted to Garibaldi. If it is significantly more or less than 50 per cent it is likely that the question is not being done justice.

---

*Source-based questions on 'Garibaldi and Italy'*

### 1  The appearance of Garibaldi
Read carefully the description of Garibaldi, given on page 59, and study the portrait of Garibaldi, reproduced on page 60. Answer the following questions:
a)  Which source is more likely to portray Garibaldi accurately, the pen-portrait or the print? Give reasons for your answer.
b)  To what extent are the two sources in agreement? Support your answer with evidence.
c)  What is the writer of the description's opinion of Garibaldi? Support your answer with evidence.

### 2  The entry of Victor Emmanuel and Garibaldi into Naples
Read carefully the extract from the account by a member of staff at the French Embassy, given on page 67. Answer the following questions:
a)  What two aspects of the entry into Naples does the writer of the

account suggest caused Victor Emmanuel offence?

b)   What suggestions are made about the relationship between Victor Emmanuel and Garibaldi?

c)   What is the writer's opinion of Victor Emmanuel? Support your answer with evidence.

## 3  The Garibaldini

Read carefully the account of the Garibaldini, given on page 70. Answer the following questions:

a)   Of what elements of the informality of the Garibaldini is the writer of the account critical? Explain your answer.

b)   On balance, is the account critical or approving of the Garibaldini? Explain your answer.

c)   What advantages did the informality of the Garibaldini give them over regular troops of the time?

# CHAPTER 4

# Napoleon III and Italy

## 1 Napoleon III of France

The family of Napoleon Bonaparte, Napoleon I, were exiled from France by the Vienna Settlement of 1815. Some of them were in Italy during the winter of 1830–31. Louis-Napoleon Bonaparte, nephew of Napoleon I, became involved there in a wild and foolish scheme to capture the Pope's castle of Saint Angelo. He led a conspiracy which planned to proclaim his cousin, the son of Napoleon I, as King of Italy. As his cousin was a prisoner of the Austrians, Louis-Napoleon would rule as regent on his behalf. The secret was not well kept and the authorities had little difficulty in uncovering the plot and arresting the conspirators. Louis-Napoleon was expelled from Rome and went to join the rest of the family in Florence, where he immediately became enmeshed in another conspiracy, organized by Menotti, in Modena and the Papal States.

At this time Louis-Napoleon was a young man of 22, inexperienced and full of impractical dreams and schemes, but genuine, if vague, liberal sympathies. The conspiracies of 1830–1 mark the beginning of his love affair with Italian nationalism, and although his actions often resulted from a mixture of motives, some of them selfish, his wish to help the Italians always remained sincere. In the end it was with his assistance that Italian freedom was achieved. Although in 1849 no one could have foreseen it.

* In March 1849 the Roman Republic was proclaimed, with Mazzini as its main administrator and Garibaldi as its military leader. The Pope, who had taken refuge in Naples, appealed to the Catholic Powers of Europe for help. Decisive action came from Louis-Napoleon, recently elected President of the French Republic. He knew that the Austrians, already occupying Tuscany and the northern part of the Papal States, would soon be threatening Rome itself, and there was no time to lose if he was to benefit from the situation. He wanted the credit of restoring the Pope, and the approval of the Church which would go with it. He may also have hoped to be able to arrange some sort of compromise between Pius IX and the Roman Republic.

The French Assembly agreed to the plan of providing an expeditionary force to Rome, and 10 000 troops set sail in April. Their commander was well received on landing near Rome, and expected the same welcome from the citizens of Rome. He was not at all prepared for the resistance organized by Mazzini and Garibaldi (see page 63). A Bonaparte could not begin his Presidency with a military defeat, and so Louis-Napoleon, after a temporary armistice, reinforced the French army. The army, now over 20 000 strong, attacked the outskirts of the city at the beginning of June and a month later the city surrendered. It was quickly restored to reactionary government by representatives of the

Papal Curia, while the French stood by. Whatever Louis-Napoleon's intentions, he had merely restored the status quo in Rome.

\* In December 1852 he assumed the title of Emperor Napoleon III. Although he declared that France wanted only peace, he soon found himself fighting against Russia in defence of Turkey in the Crimean War of 1854. Among France's allies was Piedmont, and, when the war ended in January 1856, Cavour had a seat at the Peace Conference in Paris. This brought him into direct contact with Napoleon III, with important long term effects for them both. After the Conference was over, they kept in touch through mutual friends, Napoleon's nephew, Prince Jerome, their doctor, Conneau, Cavour's private secretary, Nigra, and the young and beautiful Countess Castiglione.

\* On more than one occasion during the 1850s, Napoleon spoke to Cavour of 'doing something for Italy'. It is difficult to know exactly what he had in mind, for his reasoning was not always straightforward. The usually accepted interpretation of his words is that he wished as part of his anti-Austrian policy to drive Austria out of northern Italy, leaving the way clear for an extension of French influence through a client state, Piedmont. An equally good case can be made out for Napoleon as a romantic but sincere supporter of the Italian national cause. After all in 1830 he had been a *Carbonaro* or something very like it. Again his reasons for intervention in Italy may have been influenced by family tradition, part of the Napoleonic legend. Although he had none of the soldierly qualities, the ruthless determination or gifts of leadership of his imperial predecessor and uncle, Napoleon I, he apparently saw himself as a leader of 'the peoples' of Europe in their search for freedom and national identity.

What he meant by 'Italy' is another question. Many historians argue that before 1861, 'Italy' meant northern Italy, the equivalent of the Napoleonic 'Kingdom of Italy', and that Napoleon III would in any case not have wanted the whole Italian peninsula united into a single kingdom, for such a united neighbour might represent a threat to France.

Napoleon's plans were always fluid, complex and devious, capable of change at a moment's notice, and, because they were also secret, extremely difficult to unravel. It seems fairly certain that as far as Italy was concerned, they were based on the expulsion of the Austrians and the setting up of an enlarged Piedmont as part of the extension of French influence. The new super-Piedmont would be large enough to be a useful ally for France but not large enough to have independent policies or to resist French demands to annex Savoy and probably Nice as well. Central Italy would either be part of the new Piedmont or be a separate French client state under a pro-French ruler, such as one of Napoleon's cousins. Naples and Sicily would also be put under control of yet another cousin, while the Pope would be persuaded to agree to the new arrangements by being made President of an Italian Federation. Everyone would be satisfied; Italian nationalists by the removal of the Austrians; liberals by the abolition of the old autocratic governments; Victor Emmanuel and Cavour by the expansion of Piedmont; the clergy by an increase in the Pope's temporal power; French nationalists by the acquisition of new territory and the replacement of Austrian influence by that of France, and the Bonapartes by an extension of family power and prestige.

\* Napoleon was triggered into action in January 1858 when an attempt was made on his life. A group of four Italians, led by Count Felice Orsini, was responsible. Orsini had been an exile in London, where he had had three large bombs specially made for him. The four plotters took the bombs with them from London to Paris via Brussels, by train, completely outwitting the French police, who had been tipped off that they would be arriving by road. The bombs were thrown at Napoleon and the Empress Eugénie as their coach arrived at the opera. Eight people died and about 150 were injured.

Orsini was apparently motivated by the idea that if he killed Napoleon a republic would be restored in France, and that a republic would come to the asistance of Italy. At his trial, a letter was read out in which Orsini appealed to Napoleon to help Italy achieve independence. He was promised the blessings of 25 million citizens if he did so. There is some evidence that Napoleon himself encouraged Orsini to write the letter, and he certainly arranged for its later publication. Whether the letter was stage managed by Napoleon to give him an excuse to act, or whether it was the genuine plea from a patriot sentenced to death, is open to question.

\* Napoleon moved quickly into action. He began by meeting Cavour at Plombières, a French spa town on the border with Switzerland, on 21 July 1858 and they discussed ways to provoke Austria into war. If it could be done in a non-revolutionary way, Napoleon agreed to support Piedmont wholeheartedly, although both accepted that none of the burden of the war would fall on France, for Piedmont could only provide 100 000 of the 300 000 troops needed. (See page 44 for details of the decisions made at Plombières and incorporated into a secret treaty).

## a) The War of 1859

When Cavour refused to accept an Austrian ultimatum to disarm unilaterally, Austria declared war on 29 April, 1859 and advanced quickly in to Piedmont. On 3 May Napoleon fulfilled his promises to Cavour and declared war on Austria in support of Piedmont. For the first time railways were used to take soldiers to the front, but to make good use of the railways required careful organization and this was lacking in the French army. The men themselves arrived quickly in Lombardy, but their supplies did not. 'We have sent an army of 120 000 men into Italy before we have stocked up any supplies here', Napoleon telegraphed to Paris. Piedmontese plans for mobilization were even more incompetently carried out than those of the French. Fortunately for them the same was equally true of the Austrians. Lombardy was rapidly overrun by the combined French and Piedmontese armies. The Austrians were heavily defeated at Magenta on 4 June and Solferino on 24 June.

The carnage at both battles was horrific. The Austrian Emperor, Victor Emmanuel and Napoleon were all shocked at what they saw. Napoleon offered his personal linen to be torn into bandages for the wounded, but this was no compensation to his men for the fact that the official bandages, along with the other supplies, did not arrive until after the war was over.

As a military leader Napoleon was well intentioned but incompetent, and quite unable to deal with the problems which faced him after Solferino. The Austrians withdrew to strongly fortified positions. To reinforce the French army sufficiently for an attack on their defences would require time and effort. There was a danger that Prussia, already mobilizing along the Rhine, might use Napoleon's preoccupations in Italy to make an attack on France. Military and financial support from Piedmont had proved disappointing, and there was growing criticism in France of the whole Italian adventure. On top of everything, Napoleon found Cavour's activities in Tuscany very suspicious. It looked as if France was being taken advantage of in order for Piedmont to gain more than had been agreed.

For all these reasons Napoleon decided to make peace, although Venetia had not been captured as planned. He met the young Austrian Emperor at Villafranca on 11 July 1859. An armistice was signed and Victor Emmanuel accepted the terms, without consulting Cavour. Piedmont received Lombardy, although to save Austrian face it was ceded to Napoleon III and then passed by him to Victor Emmanuel. Austria kept Venetia, and therefore remained a powerful influence in Italy. As he had not fulfilled all the promises of Plombières, Napoleon could not insist that Savoy or Nice be handed over to France. Later, Victor Emmanuel and Cavour claimed that Napoleon had treacherously made peace with Austria behind Piedmont's back and had betrayed the cause of Italian nationalism, despite the fact that Victor Emmanuel (though not Cavour) had agreed to end the war and to accept the terms of the peace treaty.

## 2 The Unification of Italy

After Garibaldi's successful conquest of Sicily in July 1860 the European Powers suddenly realized that he intended to attack the Neapolitan mainland. Should he be allowed to do so?

Amidst a flurry of diplomatic activity, it soon became clear that only Britain among the Great Powers had any sympathy with Garibaldi's aims. Napoleon III was unwilling to offend Britain by intervening to stop Garibaldi, but equally did not want to see him take over Naples and threaten Rome and the Papacy. He therefore suggested to Britain the possibility of a joint naval blockade of the Straits of Messina to contain

Garibaldi on Sicily, but Britain refused. Garibaldi crossed the Straits successfully in the middle of August, meeting only token resistance from the Neapolitan navy which had already agreed with him not to fight seriously. When Cavour's army entered the Papal States on 11 September to prevent Garibaldi from reaching Rome, Napoleon had to disapprove in public of such unprovoked aggression, but circumstantial evidence suggests that he had made a secret agreement with Cavour that France would not interfere so long as Garibaldi did not reach Rome. Diplomatic relations between France and Piedmont were temporarily broken off, but this seems to have been in the nature of a gesture by Napoleon and was not to be taken seriously.

During the next decade, the problems of how to incorporate Rome and Venetia into the new Italian Kingdom were very pressing ones. Rome seemed to most Italians to be the natural capital of their country, the home of the old Roman Emperors and the symbol of past greatness. The French garrison in Rome and the Austrian occupation of Venetia were constant reminders that the work of driving out the foreigner had not been completed. Napoleon III, one way and another, was to provide a solution to the problems.

## a) Venetia

In 1866 the question of Venetia came to a head. Prussia was involved in a struggle with Austria for control of Germany. In a secret treaty with Prussia, Italy agreed that if Prussia went to war with Austria within two months, she would follow Prussia in declaring war on Austria. At the end of the war, after the defeat of Austria, Italy would receive Venetia as a reward for services rendered by creating a second front in an Austro-Prussian war.

Having made sure that Italy would gain Venetia if Prussia won, the Napoleon now had to make equally sure that the same thing would happen if Austria won. He therefore signed a secret treaty with Austria in which they agreed, that if Austria defeated Prussia, Venetia would be ceded to France, and passed on to Italy by Napoleon. In return France would remain neutral during the war. No wonder Napoleon had a reputation throughout Europe for deviousness and double dealing.

The war known in Germany as the Seven Weeks' War and in Italy as the Third War of Independence began on 14 June 1866. Ten days later Italy was defeated by Austria at the battle of Custoza, mainly because of poor leadership, but on 3 July Austria was herself defeated by Prussia at Königgratz. Austria immediately ceded Venetia to Napoleon, who quickly handed it on to Italy. Welcome as the acquisition of Venetia was to Italy, the way in which it was achieved, not by Italians, but through the Great Powers of Prussia, Austria and France was humiliating. Further humiliation followed a few weeks later when the Italian fleet was heavily defeated by a smaller Austrian fleet at the battle of Lissa. Despite this, the Peace of Prague, signed in August 1866, confirmed Italy's possession of Venetia, and brought the total unification of Italy a step nearer.

## b) Rome

Four years later, when the Franco-Prussian war broke out in July 1870, Italy remained neutral. Victor Emmanuel felt that the marriage of his daughter to Napoleon's cousin compelled him to go to the help of France, but his government thought otherwise. Napoleon needed a large army quickly and withdrew his troops from Rome very soon after the war began. The Italian government made no immediate move, but, after Napoleon had been defeated and taken prisoner by the Prussians on 1 September, they felt it safe to take action.

Victor Emmanuel sent a letter to the Pope on 8 September, asking him to reach an agreement with the government and accept the loss of his Temporal Power, which since 1849 had depended on the presence of French troops. He urged the Pope to allow Rome to become the capital of Italy and to settle for an arrangement of the kind suggested by Cavour in March 1861. This would have separated Church and State, leaving the Pope without temporal power, but with complete spiritual independence safeguarded and guaranteed by the State – the Free Church in the Free State. Victor Emmanuel wrote:

1  I, being a Catholic King and Italian, and, as such, guardian by the disposition of Providence and the national will of the destinies of all the Italians, feel it my duty to take, in the face of Europe and Catholicity, the responsibility of maintaining order in the
5  peninsula and the safety of the Holy See. . . . The Head of Catholicity surrounded by the devotion of the Italian people, should preserve on the banks of the Tiber a glorious seat independent of every human sovereignty. Your Holiness by liberating Rome from foreign troops will take from her the constant danger
10 of being the battleground of subversive parties.

Three days later the Pope replied,

1  I cannot admit the demands of your letter, nor accept the principles contained therein.

As a result the government decided to send an army of 60 000 to occupy Rome. Papal troops fought back briefly but the city was shelled by government artillery and a breach made in the walls. On 20 September 1870 Victor Emmanuel's army entered Rome. A plebiscite was held in October. Rome voted overwhelmingly for union with the rest of Italy, and became the capital city. The *Risorgimento* was coming to a triumphant close: the Italian Kingdom was complete. In the words of the

King addressing the first session of Parliament to be held in the new capital, 'The work to which we consecrated our lives is accomplished'. The only problem left was what to do about the Pope.

* Shortly before his death in 1861 Cavour had spoken of 'a free Church in a free state'. His idea had been to separate Church and state. The Pope's temporal powers would be ended and the remainder of the Papal lands absorbed into the Italian state, but the Pope would remain an independent sovereign, with his own diplomatic corps, and the Church would be guaranteed complete freedom from state interference. Pius IX had appeared at first to be ready to consider some such arrangement but soon changed his mind and brought unofficial negotiations to an abrupt end.

As temporal power began to slip from his grasp the Pope set about strengthening his spiritual power. In 1864 he published the controversial *Syllabus of Errors* which had the effect of condemning liberalism and religious toleration, and turning the Church away from the realities of the nineteenth-century world. In July 1870 the doctrine of Papal Infallibility was proclaimed by Pius IX during the General Council of the Church which met in Rome. This doctrine declared that the Pope's official statements were infallible – they could not be wrong, nor could they be altered. He was the supreme judge of truth for the Catholic world; his spiritual authority was unchallengable. It was ironic that only three months later Rome became the capital of Italy and the Pope, left with merely 109 acres, was describing himself as 'the prisoner of the Vatican', his temporal power extinguished. The Pope refused to accept the state pension offered him, excommunicated Victor Emmanuel and his government, but could not change the situation. Church and state in Italy were finally separated.

---

## Making notes on 'Napoleon III and Italy'

Your notes on this chapter should help you undertand the part played by Napoleon III of France in the unification of Italy. The following headings will help you to make clear notes:
1.    Napoleon III of France
1.1.  1830–31
1.2.  1849
1.3.  1849–56
1.4.  Napoleon's motives
1.5.  Orsini
1.6.  Plombières
1.7.  The War of 1859
2.    Unification of Italy
2.1.  1860–65

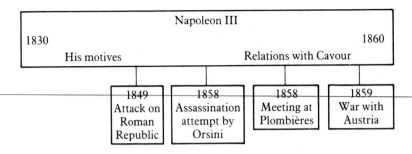

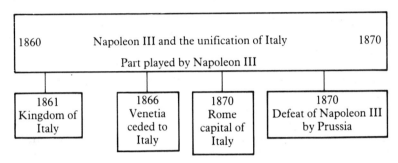

*Summary – Napoleon III and Italy*

2.2. Venetia
2.3. Rome
2.4. The Pope

---

**Answering essay questions on** '*Napoleon III and Italy*'

Much of the information in this chapter will be needed to answer general questions on the unification of Italy, particularly those of the 'Did Italy make herself' type. These are discussed on pages 92–3.

You are very unlikely to be faced with a question solely concerned with Napoleon III and Italy, but he often appears alongside an Italian in what is really a disguised 'Did Italy make herself' question. Examples are:

'What did a) Napoleon III and b) Garibaldi contribute to the unification of Italy?' (London, 1978)

'Assess the contributions of a) Cavour and b) Napoleon III to the liberation and unification of Italy' (SUJB, 1981)

Both appear to be straightforward 'comparison' questions inviting you to plan your essay by making lists of the ways in which each of the individuals contributed to unification, and then arranging the points in order of importance. Unless you are careful, however, you will fall into the trap of writing two separate and unrelated narrative accounts based on the careers of the two men. It is better to find an alternative framework within which to group your points. These could be based on their contributions to the political, military or some other broad aspect of unification. What are these 'other broad aspects of unification'? In what order would you deal with them in an essay? Why?

You may be asked to write an essay on French involvement in Italian affairs. For example:

'Why did France become involved in the movement for Italian unification, and how valuable was the help it gave?' (London, 1982)

The first half of the question is of the straightforward 'Why?' type. Plan your essay by first making a list of reasons for French involvement in Italy. Begin each with the word 'because', for example, 'because Napoleon III wanted Nice and Savoy'. Make a note of the evidence you would need to support your statements. Then arrange the statements in what seems to you the best order. What is the rationale of the order you have chosen?

The second half of the question calls for an analysis of the effects of French actions on Italian unification. Again make a list. Use two headings: 'helpful effects' and 'unhelpful effects'. For example, under the first heading you might include, the defeat of Austria in 1859 and under the second, the loss of Nice and Savoy.

When your list is complete, decide which argument is stronger – helpful or unhelpful. Which argument would you present first in your answer? Why?

---

***Source-based questions on*** '*Napoleon III and Italy*'
## 1 The Temporal Power of the Pope, 1870
Read carefully the extracts from the letter of Victor Emmanuel to Pius IX, and from Pius IX's reply, given on page 81. Answer the following questions:
a)  What were the 'demands' and 'principles contained therein' referred to by Pius IX in his reply?
b)  What are the implications of the phrase 'subversive parties', (line 10)?
c)  Victor Emmanuel knew what the Pope's response was likely to be before he wrote the original letter. Given this fact, what were likely to have been the King's motives for writing as he did?

# CHAPTER 5

# The Kingdom of Italy

What was the new kingdom of Italy like during the first decade of its existence? Cavour's successors as Prime Minister were generally undistinguished right wing politicians. None had the magic of the great figures of the *Risorgimento*. The majority were in power for only a short time, like Farini who suffered a mental breakdown, tried to knife the King and was removed from office after only three months, or Ratazzi, who became enmeshed in Garibaldi's proposed attacks on Rome in 1862 and again in 1867, as on both occasions he unfortunately happened to be Prime Minister for a few months. Yet Italian historians have argued that between 1861 and 1871 the Italian government did good solid work in establishing the new kingdom, and that in their way its members were just as important as the heroes of previous years.

The united Italy of 1861 was a constitutional monarchy, not a republic as Mazzini wished, nor a federation under the Pope as Gioberti, and later Cavour and Napoleon III had proposed. The constitution was based closely on Charles Albert's *Statuto* of 1848, and the sovereign body was the King in Parliament. But that did not mean that Italy was a democracy. Voting was restricted to males, over 25 years old, literate and tax paying – about 2 per cent of the population. Not surprisingly Parliament was conservative and unrepresentative. Strong central and weak local government on the Piedmontese model was extended after 1861 to the rest of Italy. The various legal codes which existed in each of the states were unified. A penal code based on that of Piedmont was quickly introduced everywhere, except in Tuscany which was allowed to keep its own moderate system, and in 1865 a single system of civil law was adopted throughout the country. It was similar to the *Code Napoléon*, and introduced civil marriage although divorce remained illegal. As was to be expected the unified foreign policy, foreign ministry and diplomatic service of the new Italy were based on those of Piedmont.

During the 1860s a unified Italian army was formed out of the old armies of Piedmont, Naples and the Central Italian States together with Garibaldi's 'Army of the South'. The army was modernized and reorganized on Prussian lines. Later the navies of Piedmont and Naples were integrated into a single force, although not until 1876 was any attempt made at reorganization or modernization. The state took over the control of schools and universities as part of a policy to provide a unified system of education.

## 1 North and South

The contest between north and south was the most difficult problem which the new Kingdom of Italy had to settle. Cavour himself had commented 'To harmonize the north with the south is more difficult than to fight Austria or to struggle with Rome'. The government dealt with the problem largely by ignoring it and by imposing a Piedmontese solution over the whole country, whether it was appropriate to a particular area or not. In the south it was not. The real problems in Naples and Sicily were not political so much as social and economic. The majority of the population was illiterate, lived in poverty and squalor and was near starvation. There was a growing shortage of land available to the peasants, as the great landowners continued to add to their estates. The immediate result of union with Piedmont was conscription, increased taxation, a higher cost of living and quite unsuitable and little understood new legal and administrative systems. Quickly public opinion turned against Victor Emmanuel and Piedmont, and in the early 1860s law and order broke down. Brigandage, which was endemic in the south, became uncontrollable, and civil war added to the already desperate plight of the peasant.

In Piedmont there was no attempt to understand the situation. Naples was 'rotten', the Neapolitans were 'barbarians', shiftless and idle, who brought their troubles on themselves by their laziness. The Italian government believed the south to have great wealth, just waiting for exploitation by the industrialized north and their policy of bringing the two halves of the country into direct economic competition had the effect of encouraging trade and industry in the north while worsening the situation still further in Naples and Sicily.

## 2  Mazzini's view

In 1871 Mazzini, who had hoped and worked so long for a free and united Italy, was critical.

1   The Italy which we represent today, like it or not, is a living lie. Not only do foreigners own Italian territory on our frontiers with France and Germany, but even if we possessed Trieste and Nice, we should still have only the material husk, the dead corpse of
5   Italy.
    Italy was put together just as though it were a piece of lifeless mosaic, and the battles which made this mosaic were fought . . . by foreign rulers who should have been loathed as our natural enemies. Lombardy, scene of the Great Five Days in 1848, allowed
10   herself to be joined to Italy by the actions of a French despot. The Venetians, despite their heroic defence in 1849, come to us by kind permission of a German monarch. The best of us once fought against France for possession of Rome; yet we remained the slaves of France so long as she was strong. Rome, therefore, had to be
15   occupied furtively when France lay prostrate at Germany's feet, just because we feared to raise our war cry against the Vatican. Southern Italy was won by volunteers and a real movement of the

people, but then it resigned its early promise and gave in to a
government which still refuses to give Italy a new national consti-
20 tution.
  The battles fought by Italy in this process were defeats. Custoza
and Lissa were lost because of the incompetence or worse of our
leaders. Italians are now without a new constitution that could
express their will. We can therefore have no real national existence
25 or international policy of our own. In domestic politics . . . a
narrow franchise means that we are governed by a few rich men.
. . . Ordinary people are disillusioned. They had watched . . . as
Italy, once ruler of the civilized world, began to rise again; but now
they avert their gaze from what is happening and say to themselves:
30 'this is just the ghost of Italy'.

Was Mazzini right to be so critical of the new Italy? Forty years before
he had expressed his hopes through 'Young Italy' and some at least of
these had been fulfilled. He might fret at the loss of Italian-speaking
Nice, but at least the Austrians had gone, Lombardy and Venetia were
again in Italian hands and Rome was the capital. It was the method of
their recovery which distressed him. Italy was free and united, but Italy
had not achieved this alone. Worse still, Italy had not become a republic,
and although the new kingdom was a secular one, Italian life was still
dominated by the spiritual, if not temporal, power of the Catholic
Church.
  Mazzini was justified in his comments that Piedmont had imposed
unification on Italy, with no opportunity for Italians to build a new
constitution, and right in thinking that the mass of ordinary people had
been excluded from, and did not support, the new state.

## 3 Conclusion

Whose is the credit for unifying Italy? The question has been discussed at
length by historians since 1861. The *Risorgimento*, the Italian movement
of 'resurgence' or 'national rebirth', which began in the eighteenth
century, had gained ground in the early decades of the nineteenth
century through the secret societies and under the leadership of Mazzini.
He provided the intellectual basis for the nationalist movement, as well
as the inspiration for revolution among those, like Garibaldi, with whom
he came in contact, but his writings were too academic to have a wide
readership or much popular influence.
  Italian historians have generally set out to glorify all those who took
part in unification, have played down their differences, and presented
the events of 1860–61 as the great and romantic climax to a long process
of national development, by which Italy found her national soul.
  In Italy history is often studied along with philosophy, particularly
Idealist philosophy which teaches that abstract ideas such as Italian

nationhood are the true concrete reality. This makes them suitable for historical study because in the end they will 'embody themselves' in institutions, in this case the Italian state. Their progress to this end is inevitable. Historians who accept this view must accept also that chance and accident play no part in the final outcome.

This philosophical belief, coupled with strong patriotic feelings and expressed in an emotional and rhetorical style for which Italian is entirely suitable, has meant that much Italian historical writing about the *Risorgimento* is largely incomprehensible to non-Italians, however well it is translated.

Luigi Salvatorelli, a moderate left-wing historian writing in 1943, described the *Risorgimento* as 'a fact or better a process of a spiritual character, an intimate and thorough transformation of national life . . . Italy and the *Risorgimento* have both been understood, over the centuries, as before all else as facts of consciousness, as spiritual attitudes'.*

Twenty years later, another respected Italian historian, Rodolico, wrote that 'the *Risorgimento* was a spirit of sacrifice, it was suffering in the way of exile and in the galleys, it was the blood of Italian youth on the battlefields . . . it was the passion of a people for its Italian identity.'*

British historians have seen the situation rather differently. The traditional view is that held by G. M. Trevelyan, writing in the early years of the present century. He believed that apparently conflicting forces in Italy (the moderate liberals and the republican democrats) were really complementary. They needed each other, as Cavour and Garibaldi needed each other, perhaps without realizing it, in order to unite Italy. In other words, while it was accepted that differences existed, they were dismissed as unimportant.

In 1954 Denis Mack Smith published *Cavour and Garibaldi 1860*. This influential book, based on a study of Cavour's correspondence, argued that it was just those very differences, the disputes and suspicions between the leading Italian patriots, which were the most important factors in bringing about unification. This and Mack Smith's later books, including *Italy: A Modern History*, published in 1959, ran directly contrary to the accepted Italian view of the inevitability of unification. They were the subject of fierce criticism by Italian historians, but had the effect of stimulating them to new research on the *Risorgimento*.

Stuart Woolf in his *History of Italy 1700–1860*, published in 1979, summed up current British historical thinking:

1  The new Italy emerged out of the basic conflict of the opposing patriotic forces and the personal hostility of their leaders, not out of what traditional historiography was long inclined to interpret as the complementary and implicitly harmonious roles of the four

5  'heroic' leaders – Victor Emmanuel, Cavour, Garibaldi and Mazzini – walking arm-in-arm towards a preordained unified state.

* Quoted in Beales, *Risorgimento and the Unification of Italy*.

Did the new Italy arise out of conflict? Certainly there was hostility between Cavour and Garibaldi. If Cavour had not distrusted Garibaldi and feared in 1860 that he might make himself ruler of an independent southern Italy, and that it might even be a republic, he would not have made the decisive move to invade the Papal States, which still divided Italy geographically. This invasion resulted in an open quarrel betwen Cavour and Garibaldi, between liberals and radicals on the future of the peninsula.

It has been said that Cavour united Italy in 1861 less from conviction that it was the right thing to do than from a wish to get the better of Garibaldi. Cavour did not trust Garibaldi, and continued to believe that he was still a Mazzinian at heart. Garibaldi for his part disliked Cavour and had no faith in diplomacy. He believed, even after his break with Mazzini, that Italy must be united by revolutionary means – and at once. Like a bull in a china shop, he charged into the attack on Sicily and then Naples. After his unexpected success there he planned to go on to take Venetia and Rome, without considering the political implications of what he was doing. Such action would certainly have brought intervention by France and perhaps Austria, and the new and fragile Italy could not have withstood such a crushing blow. It was Cavour's greatest contribution to unification that his invasion of the Papal States effectively prevented Garibaldi from carrying out the second part of his plan, the attack on Rome, just as it was Garibaldi's greatest contribution that he was able to carry out the first part, the conquest of Sicily and Naples, despite Cavour.

Garibaldi's readiness to surrender Sicily and Naples to Victor Emmanuel avoided civil war and left the field clear for Cavour and Piedmont to take over Italy. Was it the gesture of a great and generous man, laying the spoils of war at the feet of his King, or merely the opting out of a difficult situation, now the fighting was over? As on so many issues in the Italian question, historians are divided, but it seems probable that both Victor Emmanuel and Cavour were determined that Garibaldi's contribution was finished and that he should go, leaving them to continue in a more diplomatic way the process of unification. With no immediate prospect of further fighting Garibaldi seems to have been quite prepared, indeed anxious, to return to the simple life on Caprera.

Victor Emmanuel II, King of Piedmont and first King of a united Italy, the *Re galantuomo* (the gallant King), played little active part in the *Risorgimento*. He enjoyed great personal popularity however with his bluff and hearty manner, and perhaps because of the now largely discredited belief that he alone defied the Austrians and maintained the constitution in 1849, he is regarded by Italians as one of the heroes of the movement. Non-Italians have been less enthusiastic and are inclined to agree that his claim to fame is that he simply 'allowed Italy to create herself'. He was there at the right time and place to be the figure-head for Italian nationalism. As Garibaldi said, 'let Italy be one under the *Re galantuomo* who is the symbol of our regeneration and of the prosperity of our country'. It was who he was, not what he did, that gained Victor Emmanuel his place in *Risorgimento* history.

British historians have largely ignored the other important figure in the unification of Italy, a non-Italian, who has generally had a bad press, Napoleon III of France. Whatever his motives, the fact remains, that without his involvement and support, the Austrians would not have been driven out of Italy and an independent and united Italy would have been impossible. Many Italians must have echoed Garibaldi's words after the Peace of Villafranca 'Do not forget the gratitude we owe to Napoleon III and to the French army, so many of whose valiant sons have been killed or maimed for the cause of Italy'. (He was less enthusiastic about Napoleon and the French after the cession of Nice, his home town).

One of the few British historians to value Napoleon's part in Italian affairs, L. C. B. Seaman, believed that Italy stood for ever in Napoleon's debt for he alone made Italian freedom possible, and without him neither Cavour nor Garibaldi could have united Italy. Whether this complete unity was what Napoleon or Cavour wanted is another question; only Garibaldi had that singleminded goal.

* The new united Italy became a secular constitutional monarchy, rather than a republic or federation partly because these alternatives were discredited by 1870, but more because of the strong position of Piedmont. Piedmont, free of Austrian domination, had been the only Italian state to preserve a constitutional monarchy after the failure of the 1848 revolutions. During the 1850s Piedmont had a strong central government, a well organized administration, and an effective army, unlike any of the other states. She also had able political and military leaders, Cavour and Garibaldi, who could use diplomacy and war to best advantage. Piedmont had sufficient international status to negotiate on a near equal footing with the Great Powers, especially France whose support was to be crucial in 1859 and 1866. The National Society turned its back on its republican and revolutionary origins and campaigned strongly throughout Italy during 1859 and 1860 in favour of Piedmont, arguing that it was essential for national unity that all Italians should rally round Piedmont and her monarchy. As Piedmontese leaders played the major part in the actual process of unification, it seemed right to them that the Kingdom of Italy should have a constitution and administration as well as a legal and financial system based closely on that of Piedmont. Italy was Piedmont writ large.

This belief has been perpetuated by Italian and other historians, who have, until recently, contributed to maintaining the traditional view of the predominance of Piedmont in the story of the *Risorgimento*.

Cavour died suddenly at the early age of 51 without having had time or apparently the inclination to write his memoirs. He did, however, leave enormous quantities of letters and other papers, both public and personal. These were soon being collected and 'edited' to give a strongly pro-Piedmontese version of events by Piedmontese scholars. They used the documents to illustrate and interpret their histories of the *Risorgimento*. Where necessary, documents were suppressed or altered or even invented to give Piedmont and Cavour the dominant roles in the unification of Italy. Cavour was shown in a good light and his enemies, whether the reactionary King of Naples or the republican Mazzini, in a bad one.

British historians writing at the end of the nineteenth century were deeply influenced by this pro-Piedmontese school of thought, for they found themselves in sympathy with the moderate liberal constitutionalism of Cavour. At the same time they were attracted to the idea of the romantic national hero, and here again Piedmont provided the answer in Garibaldi.

If primary source material for understanding Cavour's intentions and beliefs was incomplete and inaccurate, so was that for Garibaldi although for different reasons. Garibaldi's own accounts of his motives and exploits were mostly written much later than the events portrayed, and are heavily fictionalized into bad novels. Even his so called *Memoirs* cover only the events up to about 1850, and were substantially 'improved' by other hands before publication. His writings are of very limited value historically in determining his part in events, particularly those of 1859–61. The new collections of his letters now being published in Italy should be more useful as they deal with occurrences contemporary with the time of writing.

It seems appropriate that the last words should be those of Massimo d'Azeglio, nobleman, writer, liberal politician, Prime Minister of Piedmont from 1849 to 1852, who did not die until 1866 and so saw unification almost completed. Often quoted is his famous remark to Victor Emmanuel, 'Sir, we have made Italy, now we must make Italians'. In other words, to impose geographical and political unity was not enough. Before a new united country such as Italy could become a nation, the inhabitants had to feel themselves to be one people, Italians.

D'Azeglio realized that this would be a slow process, and in another and much less often quoted remark, he said, 'To make an Italy out of Italians, one must not be in a hurry'. In a country with strong local loyalties, people did not automatically become Italians in 1861 or 1866 or 1870 just because they lived in Italy. They remained first and foremost Piedmontese, Neapolitans, or Venetians. Integration was going to take a long time.

---

### Making notes on 'The Kingdom of Italy'

Your notes should give you a framework for discussing the main problems faced by the new Kingdom of Italy and for assessing the relative contributions of the major actors in the drama.

The following headings will help you to make clear notes:

1. Degree of unification
2. North and South
3. Mazzini's view
4. Conclusion
4.1. Whose the credit for unification?
4.2. Why did Piedmont dominate?

---

*Source-based questions on 'The Kingdom of Italy'*

**1 Mazzini's view of the united Italy, 1871**
Read carefully the extract from Mazzini's comments on the new Kingdom of Italy, given on pages 86–7. Answer the following questions:

a) What two major criticisms does Mazzini have of the new Italy? What do these criticisms suggest about Mazzini's *values*?
b) Which of Mazzini's criticisms appears less convincing? Explain your answer.
c) What are the implications of the inclusions of the phrases 'resigned its early promise', (line 18); 'or worse', (line 22); and, 'once ruler of the civilized world', (line 28).

---

*Answering essay questions on 'The Unification of Italy 1815–71'*

On pages 3–4 you will find examples of typical questions on the general topic of the Unification of Italy 1815–71. Look again at the 'what obstacles' and 'why nationalism failed at first' questions. Go through them and note down for each one the main factors, issues or events which will provide your paragraph headings.

Take particular notice where dates are involved. The AEB 'What obstacles' question has a finishing date of 1861. This rules out any discussion of the acquisition of Venetia or Rome, whereas they would be entirely appropriate to the SUJB question, which has a finishing date of 1870. When you have decided on your paragraph headings and have made certain that they fall within the period of the question, you need to decide the best arangement for them.

A chronological order is tempting but it can be dangerous, for it is very easy to end up writing a narrative essay. It is better, therefore, to look for other ways of arranging the points you want to make.

There are several approaches available to you. You could start with the point you think is most important and continue through the list in descending order of importance. You could reverse the process, and start with the least important. Or you could group your points according to some other criterion altogether, arranging them under general historical headings, such as political, social, economic, military or religious. If you were to use this type of grouping your final paragraph would need to make clear the relative importance of the points you have made.

Choose one of the 'what obstacles' questions and try making four essay plans for it, using the four ways of grouping suggested above (chronologically, descending order of importance; ascending order of importance; general historical headings). Which plan provides the best answer? Can you think why this is so? Are your reasons likely to hold good in all questions of this general type?

The third group of general questions are the 'Did Italy make herself' type. These often embody a quotation, for example:

'Did the eventual unification of Italy bear out the prophecy of the Piedmontese King, Charles Albert that "Italy will do it alone"?' (Scottish, 1982)

' "Italia farà da sè" (Italy will make herself by herself). Did she?' (Oxford and Cambridge, 1980)

' "Italy owed her unity more to external aid than to her own endeavours". Examine critically this judgement upon the movement for Italian unification in the period 1859–70' (WJEC, 1981)

' "Italian unification was more hindered than helped by foreign intervention". Do you agree?' (Oxford, 1980)

Where you are faced with a question, like the last two examples, which draws attention to a particular factor, usually as here by a quotation, and asks you to comment on its importance, begin by deciding what the general issue is. Here it is 'Why did Italian unification come about?' The particular factor included in the WJEC question is that external aid was the most important reason.

The essay plan should follow the pattern usually employed in answering 'challenging statement' questions of this type; either, 'the factor included in the question was the most important, but other factors such as . . . were also important', or 'the factor included in the question was important, but the factors of greatest importance were . . .'

The essay could begin with a short introduction to show which of the above arguments is being used. This could be followed by paragraphs for each of the factors, starting with the one included in the question. The paragraphs could be organized in accordance with one of the four groupings discussed earlier. The essay could finish with a short conclusion, summing up the argument followed.

# Further Reading

There are a number of helpful books for students wanting to know more about this period of Italian history.
A very readable one is:

**H. Hearder** *Italy in the Age of the Risorgimento 1790–1870* (Longman, 1983)

This not only deals clearly with political events but provides useful and interesting background reading on literature and the arts, religious issues and economics and social conditions. The chapters on Piedmont and on Cavour are particularly helpful. There is also a short section on sources and on the interpretation of the evidence they provide for the unification of Italy.
A short, well documented book which deals with changing historical views on the *Risorgimento* is:

**D. Beales** *The Risorgimento and the Unification of Italy* (Allen and Unwin, 1971; new edition Longman, 1981)

The author is committed to a particular point of view, that of the historian **Denis Mack Smith**, one of whose books *The Making of Italy 1796–1870* (Macmillan, 1968), tells the story of the *Risorgimento* through documents. Another fundamental book on Italian history since 1861 is also by **Denis Mack Smith**, *Italy: A Modern History* (University of Michigan, 1979).
The emphasis is mainly on the social history of the period in:

**Professor Stuart J.** Woolf, *A History of Italy 1700–1860* (Methuen, 1979)

Included are the recent findings of Italian social historians.
Most general European histories deal very briefly with Italy, but

**J.A.S. Grenville**, *Europe Reshaped 1848–1878* (Fontana, 1976)

is very readable and has a good section on the relations between Cavour and Garibaldi.
Students who are expecting the highest grades at A level could look at Chapter 21 in

*New Cambridge Modern History, 1830–1870* Volume X, (Cambridge, 1960).

Biographies make interesting light reading and are well worth a quick skim through. The best biography of Garibaldi is probably still **G. M. Trevelyan's** classic trilogy published over seventy years ago. Written with passion and some degree of bias it provides a good 'easy read'. A more up to date, worth while biography is

**Jasper Ridley** *Garibaldi* (Constable, 1974)

For Napoleon III see **W. H. C. Smith,** *Napoleon III* (Wayland, 1972).

**Denis Mack Smith,** *Cavour* (Wiedenfeld and Nicolson, 1985)

makes use of much recent research in an up-to-date survey of Cavour's part in the Risorgimento. His Cavour and Garibaldi, (Cambridge 1954) which has been re-issued, is a scholarly comparison of the two men and their policies.

**C. Hibbert,** *Garibaldi and his Enemies* (Penguin, 1987)

is interesting and is worth dipping into to gain a flavour of the period.

**W. G. Shreeves,** *Nationmaking in Nineteenth Century Europe* (Nelson, 1984)

has been written specifically for A-level students and contains extended discussion sections in which some issues are considered in great detail.

# Sources on 'The Unification of Italy, 1815–1871'

There is no shortage of published source material in English on this subject.

The best places to start are probably:

1. **D. Beales**, *Risorgimento and Unification of Italy* (Longman, 1981), and

2. **D. Mack Smith**, *The Making of Italy 1796–1870* (Macmillan, 1968).

Other helpful publications are:

3. ed. **N. Gangulee**, *Mazzini's Selected Writings* (Drummond, 1945);

2. **F. Eyck**, *Revolutions of 1848–9* (Oliver and Boyd, 1972);

5, **S. Brooks**, *Nineteenth Century Europe* (Macmillan, 1983);

6. **G. M. Trevelyan**, *Garibaldi's Defence of the Roman Republic* (Longman, 1907);

7. **Sir John Marriot**, *Makers of Modern Italy* (OUP, 1943).

For published pictorial sources on nineteenth-century Italian history see especially:

8. **Andrea Viotti**, *Garibaldi: the Revolutionary and his men* (Blanford Press, 1979)

For a good range of illustrations on nineteenth-century European history in general see:

9 ed. **Asa Briggs**, *The Nineteenth Century* (Thames and Hudson, 1970).

## Acknowledgements
Acknowledgement is given for the use of extracts as follows:
**D. Beales**, *Risorgimento and Unification of Italy* page 9 (original source **J. de Maistre**, *Correspondence diplomatique 1811–1917*, Paris 1860)
ed **N. Gangulee**, *Mazzini's Selected Writings* pages 16–17
**F. Eyck**, *Revolutions of 1848–9* pages 21, 22, 23 (original source **L. C. Farini**, *The Roman State, 1815–50*, London 1851), 38–9
**G. M. Trevelyan**, *Garibaldi's Defence of the Roman Republic* pages 25–6, 60 (original source **Koelman**, *In Rome 1846–51*), 72 (original source **Emilio Dandolo**, *Italian Volunteers and Lombard Rifle Brigade*, Longman 1851)
**D. Mack Smith**, *The Making of Italy* pages 44–5, 46, 69, 89–90
**Sir John Marriot**, *Makers of Modern Italy* page 84

The author and Publishers wish to thank the foilowing for their permission to use copyright illustrations:
*The Illustrated London News*: cover (final repulse of the Neapolitans at the Battle of Volturno, October 1860); The British Library: page 24; Collection Bertarelli: page 40; Museo Centrale Del Risorgimento di Roma: page 61.

The author and Publishers wish to thank the following examination boards for permission to include questions:
The Associated Examining Board; Joint Matriculation Board; Oxford and Cambridge Schools Examination Board; Southern Universities' Joint Board; University of Cambridge Local Examinations Syndicate; University of London School Examinations Department; University of Oxford Delegacy of Local Examinations; Welsh Joint Education Committee; Scottish Certificate of Education Examination Board. (The essay guidance sections are the responsibility of the General Editor and have not been approved by the Boards.)

# Index